POINT & CLICK ™
INVESTOR

Seth Godin

Dearborn
Financial Publishing, Inc.

Point & Click™ Investor

This publication is designed to provide accurate and authoritative information in regard to the subject matter covered. It is sold with the understanding that the publisher is not engaged in the rendering of legal, accounting or other professional service. If legal advice or other expert assistance is required, the services of a competent professional person should be sought.

Executive Editor: Bobbye Middendorf
Managing Editor: Jack Kiburz
Interior and Cover Design: Seth Godin Productions

Published by Dearborn Financial Publishing, Inc.®

Printed in the United States of America

96 97 98 10 9 8 7 6 5 4 3 2 1

Library of Congress Cataloging-in-Publication Data

Godin, Seth
    Point & click investor / Seth Godin
      p. cm.
        Includes bibliographical references and index.
        ISBN 0-7931-2344-5 (pbk)
        1. Investments--computer networks. 2. Internet (Computer network)
        3. America Online (Online service) 4. Investments—Computer network
        resources. I. Title.
    HG4515.95.G63 1996
    025.06'3326—dc20   96-24948

Acknowledgments

This book represents the effort and cooperation of some very special people. All the folks at AOL work diligently and with foresight to build a service that is a gold mine to investors. And special thanks to our friend Marisa Paley.

At Dearborn, Bobbye Middendorf and Jack Kiburz provided the editorial support and commitment that drove the project to its completion. Ed Aviza, who knows the online world inside and out, contributed the research and assembly that make this book so useful. Julie Maner and Nana Sledzieski managed the project, handling all the design and production details quickly and skillfully while Susan Kushnick, Shelley Flannery, Bob Schnakenberg, Sidney Short, and Andrew Perlstein pulled the manuscript together. And the book wouldn't exist without the insight and vision of Karen Watts.

Contents

Preface

Have you ever dreamed of making more money but you're not sure about how to make the leap into the world of investing? Or are you an investor who's been there, done that, and is looking for new ways to get an extra edge? Whatever category you fall into, the Internet is a valuable resource you should get to know. It can link you to everything from tutorials on the fundamentals of investing to the sophisticated data used and perused by the pros. Electronic versions of the finest business and investment publications offer fast, up-to-date information and discussion groups allow fellow investors to swap insights.

Best of all, you don't have to be a technical genius to access these online resources, and you don't have to be a first-rate investor. But proceed with caution! The desire to be successful and the enthusiasm for the opportunities you encounter must be tempered with thorough research and evaluation. Every investment decision bears some degree of risk, and you are ultimately responsible for your judgment. Never be too hasty, especially online. Remember that the Internet is unregulated, and no one should receive your money unless you are sure they represent a legitimate business opportunity.

That said, ask the experts, do the research, and make decisions that match your own comfort level. Investing wisely can be the smartest thing you do with your money. And with the tools available to you on the Internet, you've never been in a better position to influence your own net worth.

WHAT'S IN *POINT & CLICK INVESTOR?*

HOLD IT! DON'T REACH FOR YOUR CHECKBOOK JUST

yet! Investing in cyberspace isn't the same as investing in a company. You aren't going to get a prospectus that tells you how to acquire shares of cyberspace for your portfolio. Rather, the purpose of this book is to introduce you to the diverse tools and vast resources available to you on the Internet. You'll also focus on the specific services offered by America Online (AOL), the largest network service provider in America today.

By using the tools available online (affectionately referred to as "cyberspace"), you can better prepare yourself to make intelligent and informed investment decisions. And everyone knows that an intelligent and informed investor is far more successful than one who isn't.

After you've read this book, you'll have a greater appreciation of the power that modern electronic communications have to provide you with timely and relevant investment information. If you learn to take advantage of this information, you will have an edge over other investors who rely on old-fashioned paper-based sources like newspapers and magazines.

How can we be so sure of that? Imagine Company X, your favorite widget manufacturer, announces early Monday morning that it expects its quarterly earnings to surpass any previous quarter's in the company's history. Suppose further that you check into your favorite news and information sites on America Online or the Internet while sipping that piping-hot cup of java each morning. Before you head for the office, you discover the amazing news that's sure to propel the stock price of Company X into the stratosphere and you place an order for a few thousand shares with your online brokerage service right at the opening bell.

Meanwhile, your unwired neighbor, who may even be reading *yesterday's* news at the kitchen table, is wondering whether or not to buy shares of Company X or is waiting for his broker to open for business. By the time he acts, the stock price has tripled in value and you, the astute and fully wired investor, are smiling all the way to the bank.

Of course, that's a slightly exaggerated scenario. But it got your attention, didn't it? And, quite frankly, it may not be so far from reality. The world of electronic media offers investors a tremendous amount of information that is usually available well in advance of comparable print media.

In addition, you will find a community of investors willing to share knowledge and information without even charging a fee for the privilege! If you learn to exploit the resources available on America Online and the Internet, you will have the best possible investment adviser ready to be summoned at your command.

What You'll Learn

 Point & Click Investor begins with a brief overview of what the Internet is and how many different things you can do on it, from sending electronic mail to finding investment ideas and stock quotes on **World Wide Web** sites.

If you're new to the "infobahn," you'll learn how to get started with America Online and how to use it to access the Internet. You'll find out how to get information on newsgroups, browse the World Wide Web, get to indexes of information, transfer files, and more.

Once you understand the basics of finding your way around online, you'll discover rich new sources of information every day.

GETTING CONNECTED

Things don't always go as planned when you work on the Internet. For no apparent reason, you may have trouble connecting to a World Wide Web site. Instead of seeing *The Wall Street Journal*'s "Money and Investing Update," you see a cryptic error message that says something like, "Server cannot be located. Try again." You do, and you get the same message.

Be sure you entered the Web address (called a "uniform resource locator" or URL) correctly. This is usually a series of characters strung together (such as http://falco.cc.ukans. edu/njs). Try to enter a different URL and see if that works. If nothing you do works, check your browser or the way your telecommunications software is configured.

If you did enter the URL correctly, then check to see if AOL is having a system problem. If it is, you'll probably get some type of specific AOL error message. If you think it may be AOL, use the online help feature so you can eliminate that possibility.

If the problem isn't you or AOL, then it may be the site itself. It may have too many people signed on when you try to connect, or it may just be shut down for maintenance—in which case you probably won't get any kind of feedback. If it's the remote site, there's not much you can do except try again later.

Detailed instructions that explain how to use AOL and the Internet to find investment information will radically change the way you manage your investment portfolio. You'll learn how much AOL has to offer the individual investor, and why services like the **Motley Fool** are so popular. You'll be guided through AOL's **Personal Finance** center, which will become your "base of operations" for discovering additional sources of investment information, including news services such as *The Wall Street Journal* and *Investor's Business Daily.*

Point & Click Investor will also show you how to look for information on the Internet, particularly on the World Wide Web and in Usenet newsgroups. If you're anything like thousands of other Web users, you'll constantly be amazed at how much information is available online and how easy it is to find it. And if you're nothing at all like the thousands of other Web users out there, you'll probably be even more astounded at the amazing and unusual tidbits you'll pick up in the remotest and most interesting corners of cyberspace!

Finally, this book provides you with the tools you'll need to find information

about the companies and mutual funds in which you plan to invest. You'll learn not only how to contact thousands of national and international companies but how to gather *specific* financial planning and manufacturing data—the kind that can give you an edge over other, perhaps less informed investors.

Why Look to AOL and the Internet for Investment Information?

 Simple. You could buy every newspaper on the stands, then go to the library and scour all the sources available. But you would still never find all the information that you can on AOL and the Internet. Even if you *could* find all the same information, it would likely be outdated in comparison. Why? Because using the Internet provides you with a fast link to thousands of information-rich locations that are all connected, and that are typically updated daily, hourly, or even by the minute! Going to one will easily lead you to another, and another, and so on.

Working with AOL and the Internet lets you search without the headaches of digging through stacks of papers and magazines and with far greater success. The growth rate of the

Internet is phenomenal. Each year thousands of businesses and investment services go online making even more company information, stock analysis, and investment wisdom available to you in the comfort and privacy of your home or office.

What Is the Internet?

 Basically, the Internet is a network of networks. A network is a group of computers that are connected to one another and can all communicate with each other. When you combine many networks by using common standards and a common protocol (the "language" used by these computers to communicate with each other), the size of the entire network grows considerably. So does the availability of information. Data on any one network or computer can be accessed by computer users at any other location, anywhere around the world!

A Quick History of the Internet

 The Internet started around 1969 with a United States Defense Department effort to create a secure communications system that could withstand a nuclear war. This system was designed to connect military contractors to one another. Eventually, as word spread about the efficiency of this system for sharing information among geographically distant locations, other interested parties, such as researchers at universities, wanted in on the connections as well.

One network led to another, and before long there were several new networks. But there was a new problem—these independent networks could not "talk" to one another, since they had yet to be connected. Even before the networks could communicate with each other, and before people on the network could share information, some kind of standard had to be designed so network traffic could be routed reliably. The Internet Protocol, or IP, was thus born, and all the networks, including ARPANET (Advanced Research Project Agency Net), MILNET (Military Net), BITNET (Because It's Time Net), and others were finally operating on the same standard.

Then, in about 1986, the National Science Foundation stepped in and united all these different networks by dedicating five supercomputers to manage all the traffic on and between networks. It wasn't official, but, with the introduction of these five computers, the Internet was born. At a growth rate of more than ten percent each month, the Internet now connects more than 10 million people in the United States alone and probably some 100 million around the world.

Who Owns It?

 The Internet is not itself comprised of the actual physical connections that exist between all these networks. Rather, it's more a set of standards and rules that people have voluntarily complied with in order to have the most efficient form of communication ever developed.

Who enforces these standards, and where do they come from? Each Internet site, such as AOL, Netcom, or The National Center for Supercomputing Applications at the University of Illinois (NCSA, where Mosaic was originally developed), has a system administrator who is responsible for making sure things at that site run smoothly. This is the person who assigns each new user his or her e-mail address (such as "jane@aol.com" or "john@uofkansas.edu") and also decides what newsgroups are accessible on the site, the hours of operation, and just about every other housekeeping task.

In turn, the system administrator looks to several informal groups, such as the Internet Society (ISOC, formed in 1992), for advice on everything from standards used in assigning names to how to manage an ever-increasing number of users. The ISOC consists of engineers, users, subgroups galore, and many others (mostly volunteers) who help keep the Internet going. There's no big corporation running things, no interference from federal, state, or local governments, and most people would prefer to keep it that way.

So, who owns the Internet? No one and everyone.

What's Out There Anyway?

 If you can imagine what you want to do and it involves information, then the odds are pretty good that you can do it on the Internet. Here's a description of some of the major uses of the Internet and how it relates to the goal of finding investment-related information online.

The number one use of the Internet is electronic mail, or *e-mail*. Just like the regu-

lar mail (now dubbed "snail mail"), an e-mail message can be sent to a person at a particular address. That person can respond by sending a message back almost instantaneously. The big difference is that e-mail is much faster than snail mail, and it rarely gets lost.

Right behind e-mail, and rapidly becoming just as popular, is the use of the *World Wide Web*, or "the Web," a hypermedia system that retrieves information from the Internet and portrays it in a graphic format. The fantastic thing about the World Wide Web (WWW), which you can reach through AOL or your own WWW browser, is that all it takes is a click of your mouse to go from one information-rich site to another, even if the sites are on opposite sides of the globe!

To search for information, you can use the amazing tool known as a **Gopher.** You can use Gopher to go to a location and, from there, point and click your way through various menus that connect you to different Internet resources. You can use Gopher to search the Internet for papers and treatises of all sorts regarding the best ways to approach investing, what to look for in stocks and

mutual funds, and how to protect yourself from scams and phony investment "opportunities."

When you find documents that are of interest to you, you can use file transfer protocol, or **FTP,** to transfer the file from an Internet site to your computer. You can also use FTP to download programs such as stock graphing and investment analysis tools that are available on a number of sites. Many of these "shareware" programs (programs you can try free of charge, and for which you pay only if you decide to keep using them) are of as good or better quality than some of the commercially available software products on the market today!

The discussion groups of yesterday are the **Usenet** newsgroups of today. A newsgroup is an electronic medium where you can exchange ideas and information. Basically, it's an "electronic bulletin board" where people can post messages. These newsgroups are invaluable for helping you dig up information about investment opportunities, and they also provide a forum in which many like-minded investors can share information, investment tips, and other useful (and sometimes not so useful) information. Many of the discussions on Usenet develop into cheerleading groups for investors in winning stocks, and support groups for those who have not done so well. If your investments have gone south, at least you may be somewhat consoled by the knowledge that you are not alone out there!

As you read through *Point & Click Investor*, you'll learn how to use AOL, how to find your way around the Internet, and how to discover that one-in-a-million stock tip you've been dreaming about! Well, at least you'll get an idea or two about what to look for next time you're possessed by the itch to increase your returns.

Can the Internet Help You Make Money?

 Quite simply, the vast amount of information available on AOL and the Internet can give you an edge over other investors who are not able to access this information as quickly or as efficiently.

The tale of the widget company may have been a bit overstated, but the message of the parable should be very clear. The world of cyberspace gives you access, from a comfortable

location in your own home, to resources and information that can help you make fully-informed, intelligent investment decisions.

From far-out opinions on Usenet to company home pages with the latest product announcements, to the Securities and Exchange Commision's database of corporate earnings, to real-time stock quotes, the scope of knowledge within your reach is incredible. Of course, the way you manage this information, and whether you act on the information in a way that will increase your bottom line, depends completely on your own ability to make good judgments about the value of the information you've uncovered. The tools you need are available out there—it is up to you to use them to your advantage.

How to Use This Book

 Point & Click Investor will provide you with hands-on experience to get you up and running right away in your efforts to find useful investment information. If you are already online, you can skip chapter one and dive right into the resources available on AOL by reading over chapter two. However, you may want

to take a moment to consider these suggestions:

- Review the Contents to familiarize yourself with the book's scope. Browse sections you may be comfortable with and explore any areas you find interesting.

- Prepare for a dynamic experience. The Internet, and especially the World Wide Web, is an ever-changing entity. What you find there today may be gone or changed tomorrow, and what's not there yet may one day appear. Addresses change, sites are redesigned, and so

HOW DO YOU PICK A WINNING INVESTMENT?

Many people think of "playing the stock market," as if investing were a game. There are risks involved, but selecting a winning investment should be more than just a gamble. Remember that an investment is a considered decision to place your financial resources in a company— after considering its success, or likely success. This simple method is known as the *value approach* to investing, and is used by such successful investors as Warren Buffett and Peter Lynch. In general, the theory is that if a company is successful, experiences growth, and is well-managed over the long term, it is likely that the stock price will increase in value.

on. If you go to a particular home page and find that it doesn't appear as described in this book, don't despair. You're probably still in the right place. Just continue reading and clicking along.

- Don't worry if your Web search results differ from the examples shown here. Chances are the lists have evolved, so you'll find even more helpful data.

- Be aware that screen images and step-by-step instructions may differ slightly between PC and Macintosh versions of AOL. This book demonstrates the PC instructions, but most should work on a Mac, as well.

- Keep in mind that anything you can access through AOL's World Wide Web browser can also be accessed through other commercial services such as CompuServe and Prodigy, or through any of the other browsers that are available, like Netscape and Mosaic.

AMERICA ONLINE AND THE INTERNET

AMERICA ONLINE (AOL) IS THE PLACE TO START EXPLORING

the world of online investment opportunities. To make sure you get off on the right foot, this chapter addresses the investor who is not currently an AOL user and who doesn't have any experience with the Internet. You'll learn how to sign up on AOL, how to connect to the Internet, and how to use different Internet tools to assist you in your quest for data.

Installing AOL

 AOL is one of the many different commercial online information providers. What sets it apart from the others, however, is that it is currently the largest, with over 5 million subscribers. And the number is increasing every day. What this means for you is that the amount and the value of the content available will continue to increase and improve.

To begin using AOL, you must first install the software. Use the software we've given you with this book, or call AOL. There number is (800) 827-6364 and request a free startup kit. Be sure to ask for the correct size and type of media you want to use, such as 3.5" disks or CD-ROM. Also specify whether you are working on a Macintosh or IBM-compatible computer.

AOL software is often in any one of several different popular computer magazines, such as *Computer Life* or *PC Novice.* The AOL software comes in its own cardboard jacket, packaged along with the magazine, which is contained in a large plastic envelope. In addition, AOL is often pre-loaded on new computer systems, such as those you can purchase from companies like Dell, Compaq, and Acer.

Finally, you can probably get it from a friend. AOL, like most online information providers, is now sending the software directly to homes, without it even being requested. If you're on the right mailing list, then you know what we're talking about, since you've probably already received multiple copies.

A note of caution: Be sure that the version of AOL you get is the latest one. The version is usually printed on the disk label. Call AOL customer service at (800) 827-6364 to verify the latest version number. The instructions noted here may change as AOL and other online sites are updated.

Installing AOL is easy:

1. Insert the America Online disk or CD-ROM into the appropriate drive. If you are using **Windows 3.1,** be sure that the **Program Manager** window is visible.

2. From the Program Manager menu, click on **File,** then click on **Run.** You will see the Run dialog box. If you are using **Windows 95,** click on the **Start** menu and click on **Run**.

3. In the Run dialog box, type a:\setup.exe and press **Enter.** If you placed the AOL disk in drive B, then type b:\setup.exe and press **Enter.** AOL may search to see if you have a previous version of the software already installed and for information about your modem. Respond to the prompts that AOL presents.

4. Click on **Install.** AOL begins the installation process, which will take a few minutes while all the files are transferred. At the end of the installation, you will see the AOL group icon.

5. Click on **OK,** then double-click on the **AOL** icon and you'll see the

Welcome to America Online! screen, with information about what the service offers. If the sign-on information is accurate for your situation, click on **Yes.** If not, then click on **No** and make any necessary corrections. When you click on **OK,** AOL will use a special 800 number to help you select the correct access telephone number for your location.

6. Click on **Continue.**

To enter information about yourself:

1. Enter your area code and press **Enter** or click on **Continue.**

2. From the list of local phone numbers that AOL has available in your area, click on the one you want to use, and then click on **Select Phone Number.** If you have several options, click on the one with the maximum speed your modem can accommodate.

3. Repeat Step 2, this time selecting an alternative access number just in case the first phone number is busy or not working. Click on **Select Phone Number** and click on **Continue**.

4. To confirm that the phone numbers dis-

played are the ones you want, click on **Enter** after each. AOL will hang up and redial, using the primary number you selected to connect you to AOL.

5. Enter the registration number and password that came with the installation disk and click on **Enter.** Be sure to type correctly, and use the backspace key to delete errors. You can move from field to field using the tab key.

6. Fill in the rest of the registration information required and click on **Continue.**

7. Click on **Continue** until you get to the **Billing Options** screen, where you should double-click on one of the credit card options or select other billing options, if appropriate.

8. Enter the card number, expiration date, and bank name. Also enter the exact way the first and last name appear on the card. Click on **Continue** when you are finished. Confirm the address where your credit card company will send statements.

9. Read the AOL legal disclosures and click on **I Accept.**

10. Type in the screen name and password.

Your screen name is the name that you will use when you connect to AOL. It will also be the address that AOL uses to direct e-mail and other online transactions to your mailbox, and it will be your "handle" or "pen name" while you are online.

Screen names must be at least three characters and not more than ten. Because so many people are using AOL, don't be surprised if your first choice for a screen name is already being used. Passwords need to be at least four, but no more than eight, characters in length. AOL will ask you to enter your password twice to confirm it. When you are finished, click on **Enter.**

11. Click on **Enter** for the next several screens, and then select **Enter America Online.** Once you connect, you'll see the AOL opening screen. Since this is the first time you are connecting, it may take several minutes for AOL to download the artwork it uses in its opening screens. Take your time and watch as you enter this fascinating and fun world.

AOL Main Screen

Any time you want to start AOL, just double-click on the **AOL** icon in the AOL group if you are using Windows 3.1. In Windows 95, use the **Explorer** to go to the **AOL25** folder and double-click on the AOL icon. If you want, you can place the AOL icon in the **Startup** group (in Windows 3.1 or Windows 95) so it begins each time you start Windows. You can also place it on the **Start** menu in Windows 95 so it is easily accessible, but it will not automatically start when Windows 95 does.

Now That You're Signed On

 There are four basic skills you need to master when using AOL:

- Keywords
- Help options, in case you get lost

- Electronic mail
- Connecting to the Internet

Each skill is covered here as well as an introduction to some of the side trips you'll enjoy.

Using Keywords

 Keywords allow you to jump from one location to another on AOL. For example, when you enter the Keywords "Historical Quotes" and then press **Enter,** AOL takes you to a stock quote and graphs screen. The same is true for "MTV" (to get to the Music Television screen), "MAD" (to get to the *MAD Magazine* screen), and, of course, "Internet" (to get to the Internet screen). Here's what you do:

1. From the AOL menu, click on **Go To,** then click on **Keyword,** or

use the **Ctrl+K** key combination. There's also a button on the toolbar that will take you to the Keyword entry screen.

In a moment you'll see a Keyword entry dialog box.

2. Type the Keyword and press **Enter.** In a moment you'll be connected to the location you specified.

What happens if you don't even know where to start or what keyword to enter? Type a term that's as close as possible to what you want, then click on **Search.** AOL will search for keywords in its database that match the term you entered. Let's say that you want to find information about personal finance. Enter the words "Personal Finance" into the search entry box and click on **Search.** AOL will return a long list of keyword topics that you can use to get to various areas that may interest you.

You can either double-click on any of these entries or highlight the entry and click on **View Description** to learn more about the listing. Any one of these can lead to information about investments or finance. Don't worry about trying to guess the perfect keyword. You can enter anything that is related to your topic of interest; chances are that AOL will return at least a few useful entries.

Help Options

 Everyone needs help sometimes. AOL offers various levels of help, all of which can be identified from the **Member Services** screen. You can get online help from other members and from the AOL technical support staff, or offline from customer service. The best place to start is with the Keyword "Help." You'll be presented with an extensive menu of options, which is broken into two categories, online and offline.The type you select depends on the way you like to work and how badly you need help.

Clicking on the **Tech Support Live** option provides you with direct, realtime feedback from someone at AOL who is actually there in person. You type in a question, and the AOL representative responds with an answer. At night, this real-time help system gets very busy. In that case, you may want to use one of the offline features.

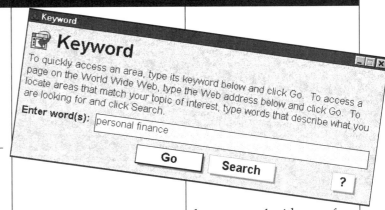

There are several ways you can obtain help offline, and all of them are explained on the help screen. Directions are given for connecting to a separate AOL bulletin board, a fax-on-demand help system, or the menu bar. In order to speak with an AOL representative by phone, you are instructed to call customer service at (800) 827-6364 and ask to

be connected with one of their technical specialists.

Using AOL E-Mail

 E-mail is the most frequently used feature of the Internet. It's easy, convenient, fast, and inexpensive. What more could you want? AOL's e-mail system is much like any other Windows-based mail program, and using it takes

The keyword search for "Personal Finance" returns a list of personal finance sites.

three steps:

1. Starting the mail function

2. Composing the message you want to send

3. Sending the mail

Being able to communicate electronically can be a great advantage when you are trying to get information from other investors, or from a company whose stock you may want to purchase. Some companies may be willing to e-mail financial information or an investor's kit to you upon request. You can also keep in contact with other investors or with brokers, if they are online.

In addition to being able to send messages through AOL, you can forward a message you receive to other Internet users, send mail to users outside of AOL (such as those who use CompuServe and MCI mail), and mail other documents as an e-mail message.

Starting, Composing, and Sending Mail

 It's easy. Here's how to compose and send a message to another investor whose CompuServe account is 12345.678@ compuserve.com. Assume that you've found a copy of Company X's most recent quarterly report and your online friend has asked you to e-mail him a copy.

Start by first going to the **Mail** feature on the AOL **Main Menu** opening screen. If you are not there, you can usually click on a **Go To Main Menu** option in whatever screen you are in. Then:

1. Click on **Post Office** on the Main Menu. When you do this, you'll see

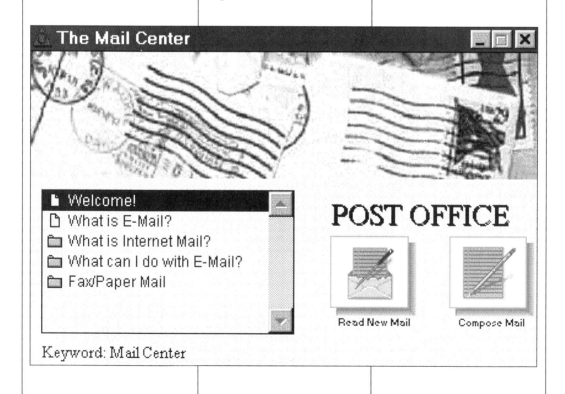

the Post Office opening screen.

2. Click on the **Compose Mail** icon, and you'll see the Compose Mail screen.

3. Enter the address to which you want to send the message. In this example, it's 12345.678@compuserve.com. Use the **Tab** key to move to the next field in the Compose Mail window and to move to any other field.

4. If you want, enter another address in the cc: area indicating to whom you want a copy of the message sent.

5. Enter a subject for the message.

6. Compose the message in the large message area.

7. Click on **Send.** The mail is on the way!

You may have noticed that in the Compose Mail window you can also schedule the mail to be sent later (perhaps after you call and tell the other person that mail is coming), attach a document, or use an address that was stored in the Address Book. To add names to your address book, click on the **Address Book** icon on the Compose Mail screen, or click on **Mail,** then **Edit Address**

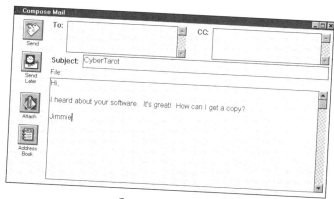

Compose Mail screen

Book from the AOL menu. When you save names in your address book, you'll save time later when you are composing messages, and you won't have to remember all those e-mail addresses.

To save online time and money, you can compose mail messages offline, and send and receive mail using **FlashSessions.** For details, click on **FlashSessions** from the **Mail** item on the menu bar. When you've set up your options for FlashSessions, you can compose a message, then click on the **Send Later** button to store the mail for later delivery.

E-Mail Addresses

 Anyone who uses e-mail on any system has an address. On AOL, your address is simply your **screen name,** or **user name.** However, if

WHAT'S IN A NAME?

The Internet uses rules to assign an address to a user, be it a person, a company, or the federal government. One of the ways you can tell what type of organization (otherwise known as a "domain") a user belongs to is to look at the last three characters in the address, called the extension. Here's a list to help you identify where the message might be coming from:

.com—commercial (aol.com is from America Online)

.edu—educational (falcom.cc.ikans.edu is from the University of Kansas)

.gov—government (whitehouse.gov is from the White House)

.mil—military (gordon.army.mil is from the Army)

.org—miscellaneous organization (ahkus.org is from the Chinese Poem Exchange Network)

.net—network resources and information centers (archie.sura.net is from a network indexing system)

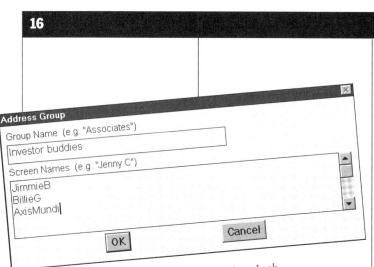

Adding a name to your address book

you want someone at another service, such as CompuServe, to be able to send mail to you at AOL, they will have to address mail to you in a format that can be routed through the Internet.

Your e-mail address for Internet users, or users of other services who want to send e-mail to you through the Internet, consists of your screen name, the "@" symbol, and finally "aol.com". For example, if your screen name is Sethg, then someone on another service can send you e-mail by addressing the message like this:

Sethg@aol.com.

Simple, isn't it? Of course, you have to know the user name or address before you can send mail. The best way to find a user's name is by using the phone and calling him or her, or by retrieving it from an earlier message. Once you know a person's e-mail address, you can save it in the **Address Book,** and you won't have to worry about remembering it again! To add a name to the address book, you need to enter a **Group Name** and **Screen Names.** You can create entries for individuals by entering only one name in the Screen Names list.

Reading Your Mail

 Sending mail is an essential skill when you are online. So is being able to read it. When you sign on to AOL and you have mail, AOL indicates that on the opening screen. If you have sound on your computer,

you'll even hear a friendly computer voice tell you, "You've got mail!" To read it:

1. Click on the **You Have Mail** icon on the main screen.

   Your toolbar also has a **mailbox** icon that will show a red flag when you have new mail.

2. Double-click on the new message you want to read, or click to highlight the message and then click on the **Read** button. The contents of the message appear on the screen.

The mail screen tells you the subject of the mail (entered by the sender), the date and time the mail was sent, who sent it, and to whom the mail was sent. Finally, there's the message itself and AOL network information at the bottom of the screen. You have several options in this window, such as replying to the sender, forwarding on to someone else, and replying to other people associated with the message (such as other people to whom the message was sent).

Replying to Mail

 Most of the time, you'll want to reply only to the individual who sent you the original mail. This is done easily enough simply by clicking on the **Reply** button in the same window in which you read the mail. In effect, when you reply, you are composing a message. The nice thing is that AOL already knows who the mail is going to, so you don't need to fool around with addresses. Now just enter the message, and click on **Send** when you are finished. The mail will be there in no time.

Mail and List Servers

 There's another way of using e-mail that you need to know about so you can keep current on the latest investment news and information: using a mailing list, and joining a **listserve discussion group.** A listserve group is an automatic depository for information. If you subscribe to it, everything that the list manager receives, you will receive by e-mail as well. There are thousands of lists, and you can usually tell by the list title what type of information is exchanged.

How to Join a List

 You join a list by sending a specific message to the list administrator. For example, here's what you would do to join the eINVEST Electronic Investor mailing list.

1. Click on **Mail,** then **Compose Mail** from the AOL menu, or press **CTRL-M,** or click on the **Compose Mail** icon on the AOL toolbar.

2. Type the word "listserv@" followed by the address of the list. Notice that there is no "e" on the end of the word "listserv." In our example, the address you need to type is:

   listserv@vm.temple. edu

3. In the message area, type the specific message that the list calls for. AOL also requires that you enter something in the **Subject** box, so you can probably just enter the same text as the message. In the eINVEST example, the message requires that you enter your name after the subscribe message. If your name were Seth Godin, the message you'd need to enter would be:

   subscribe e_invest Seth Godin

4. Send the message.

The subscribe message will be sent to the list administrator, and you will begin receiving every mail message that is sent to the list site. It's essential that all you include in your mes-

sage is what the list calls for and no more. Otherwise, the automated system that sends you the mail received by the site will become confused, and you probably won't receive anything.

How to Unsubscribe from a List

 It's conceivable that you will get hundreds of messages per day, depending upon how active a list is, so you have to check your mail regularly and clean out your mailbox to make room for new messages. It's also possible that you will want to unsubscribe or stop receiving messages from a list server. If this is the case, follow these steps:

1. Type the address of the list prefaced by the "listserv" command.

2. In the message area enter "unsubscribe."

3. Send the message. This should remove you from the list.

Be Careful with E-Mail!

 There's no doubt that there are significant advantages to using e-mail rather than regular snail mail, since it's cheaper and more reliable. But there are some drawbacks you should be aware of. First, there's little privacy or security. It's not all that difficult to access other people's e-mail, especially if you are using a commercial service. So you should never send anything through e-mail that you wouldn't want everyone in your office to read.

Second, e-mail can be easily falsified. Just take a look at any of the screens we've shown you in this chapter. All it takes is a screen capture program and a word processor to duplicate any of it.

Finally, there's no paper trail or tangible record of what happened throughout a transaction unless someone saves all the e-mail between parties (which rarely happens). With no hard copy, it's difficult to establish proof of what occurred. If you are sending important messages back and forth, it may be a good idea to print your messages so you can save a record of your correspondence. Use e-mail and have fun. Just remember its limitations.

Using the AOL Internet Connection

 Not only does AOL provide a tremendous selection of services and information that is available only to its customers; it also provides you with a direct ramp

TEN INTERNET COMMANDMENTS

Although these didn't come down from a mountain on stone tablets, they're good advice. Read them and try to adhere to them.

Commandment #1. Be sure you're connected.

If you're a beginner, you might not actually be connected to the Internet, even if you think you are. If you're an AOL user, you'll probably hear some type of voice message saying, "Welcome." If you don't hear the welcome, you may not have installed sound when you installed AOL. You can go back and re-install it easily. If you don't see any activity on the screen, exit AOL and try again. In some circumstances you may have to reboot your computer to clear the modem connection before you can connect again.

Commandment #2. Once you press the key, it's over.

There's no recalling keystrokes. Once you press that enter key or execute a command such as Send Mail, it's done. This is especially important when it comes to e-mail. Once you send an angry letter, it may be very difficult to go to the mailbox and fish it out. Be extra careful and extra sure of what you want to say before you send it electronically.

Commandment #3. Typing counts, and sometimes case does, too.

One of the idiosyncrasies of some of the operating systems on the Internet and computers connected to it is that uppercase (e.g., A, B, C) and lowercase (e.g., a, b, c) have different meanings. Many Internet connections require you to use uppercase to sign on. If your password is "Sara," then "sara" may not work. Also, type carefully. The Internet often demands long names and addresses. It's easy to type user name @ukans.cc.eud, instead of user name @ukans.cc.edu and then spend the next hour trying to figure out why you couldn't connect.

Commandment #4. Be flexible about when and how you use the Internet.

Internet sites may be very busy places, especially if you try to locate or download a file during regular business hours. If you choose to work during these hours, you'll have to be patient, because it will take longer to do almost everything. Better yet, work on your Internet e-mail and other Internet activities after dinner, or during the late evening hours, or even on the weekend—when institutional, research, and business users are often not online. But remember, the Internet is a global community, so users are in many different time zones.

Commandment #5. Not all Internet sites are created equal.

Some Internet connections offer text only, while some offer everything you could imagine, including sound and video clips. You never know what a site offers until you visit it, so be flexible. And experiment with sites that seem only onto the Internet. And the only cost is your membership in AOL. Getting to the Internet through AOL is as easy as starting any Windows program. You just click on the **Internet** button on the main menu. You can also click on the **Internet** button on the toolbar at the top of the screen.

When you do this, you'll jump right to AOL's **Internet Connection** opening window. When you get there, you'll see AOL's Web browser. The Web browser is a tool that allows you to search through the World Wide Web to find information that might be of interest to you. These days, the Web is likely to be the primary source of information that you will want to explore on the Internet because the Web has grown tremendously over the past few years. It will continue to grow as more and more companies make information available on their own Web sites.

Using the World Wide Web Browser

 You already know that the Internet is a network of networks. The World Wide Web (WWW, or more simply, the Web) is a collection of documents on those networks that are linked to

remotely applicable. You might be surprised!

Commandment #6. There's more stuff out there than anyone can know about.

When you get on the Internet for the first time, you probably won't be able to contain your enthusiasm. That's great, but don't get carried away. There are thousands and maybe even millions of files and resources out there for you to access and use. It will take you months to find out everything, and more information is being added every day. Take in a little at a time and be successful, rather than trying to surf all over the Net and getting frustrated in the process. You might also want to keep a pencil and paper handy so you can record your travels and stops along the way.

Commandment #7. Be considerate of others and play by the rules.

Without rules or etiquette to follow, it's likely that the Internet would self-destruct, as would any large organization that has no guidelines and no one in charge. For that reason, a set of informal and unenforced rules have evolved. See the sidebar on Netiquette for some of these rules.

Commandment #8. Practice, practice, practice.

The more you practice, the more you will learn and the more useful the Internet will be for you. When you first get started, however, take your time and limit your efforts to an hour or less. This will prevent fatigue and frustration. A side benefit of practicing is finding new Internet resources (such as newsgroups or programs) and shortcuts that aren't documented.

Commandment # 9. Be patient with yourself.

Learning to use the Internet is not like learning to use a new word processor or play a new game. There is little documentation and no single program that runs everything. If you have difficulty at first, don't quit. Read as much as you can about the Internet. Talk to oth-ers, and you will eventually find yourself successful. Above all, explore.

Commandment #10. Ask others for help, and help others.

A tremendous amount of valuable information comes from other users, rather than documentation such as user manuals, write-ups, and technical papers. You can learn a significant amount by reading the documentation for an application or a system (and even by reading some books, too!). You can also learn all types of other important tips, tricks, and clues from that person sitting next to you in the computer lab or a good friend who's been around the block a few more times than you have. Ask politely for help and pay back that debt by helping others when you learn new and interesting things.

one another. Clicking on a word, icon, or picture in one document can take you to another document in a matter of seconds, even if that document is stored on a computer on the other side of the globe!

The Web consists of what are called distributed hypertext documents, more commonly known as home pages, that contain "hot links" from one home page to another. The only way you can see these pages is by using a browser, like the one that AOL provides. Almost all information providers offer browsers of one sort or another. In addition, there are many companies that are only in the browser business, such as Netscape and Mosaic.

Once you establish an Internet connection, any of these will do just fine. But if you are using a commercial service provider, such as AOL or CompuServe, then you will probably use the one that they provide, as is demonstrated here.

Using the AOL Browser

 To enter the AOL browser, click on the **World Wide Web** icon on the Internet Connection window. You can also enter "WWW" in the Keyword entry screen to jump directly to the

browser. When you do this, you will see the AOL **Welcome to the Web** home page, your starting point for exploring the World Wide Web.

The AOL browser has several buttons that you'll want to become familiar with, since this is the primary tool you'll be using to surf the Net and find information about companies and other possible investment opportunities. The buttons on the toolbar at the top of the screen are the same as the buttons for any other AOL window.

The **Back** button takes you to the previous page in your sequence.

The **Reload** button reloads the current page. You may want to do this if you have clicked on something on the page and changed the information contained on the page, or if the page gets "stuck" and doesn't display completely.

The **Forward** button takes you to the next home page on your list.

The **Favorite Places** button lets you recall a list of all those home pages you want to revisit. Instead of having to enter the address for the home page, you can just click on Favorite Places and then click on the home page you want to visit. This

is similar to the Address Book feature for e-mail. The **Prefs** button lets you set preferences for using the browser, including such features as whether you want to show graphics (a no-no for computers equipped with very slow modems), or load graphics in compressed form. This option lets you see the graphics, but reduces the image's quality a bit so it displays on your screen faster.

The **Home** button lets you return to your home page (Click on **Prefs** on the Web Browser screen to input your default home page address).

The **Help** button gets you help on using the AOL browser.

Finally, the **Stop** button stops the browser from loading a home page, useful when the page you are loading is gigantic and you want to cancel the action, or if you realize too late that you've gone to the wrong site.

Home Pages

 Below every browser button is the location or address for the site's home page (the Uniform Resource Locator or **URL**). For example: http://www. sec.gov is the address for the Securities and Exchange Commission's (SEC) home page. Once you know the URL for a home page and you have your Web browser loaded, all you need to do is enter the URL in the Keyword entry screen or in the location area at the top of the screen and press **Enter.** AOL does the rest.

As you may have noticed, all URLs begin with the letters "http," which stands for *hypertext transfer protocol*. It is the system, or set of rules, used by the Web to transfer information from the Internet to your computer. Typing URLs is no fun, and often they are so cryptic that you can't tell what company or organization the URL belongs to. It's probably obvious that http://www.ibm.com is the URL for IBM, but many other URLs are not so easy to decipher.

One of the lessons you'll learn about entering URLs is that you have to type accurately when entering them. If the URL address contains capital letters, enter them as such, since URLs can be case-sensitive, and case counts. If you enter the URL incorrectly, the browser may not know where you want to go, and you'll get an error message like:

404 NOT FOUND - The

requested URL was not found on this server.

Or in other words, retype the URL and try again. Unfortunately, this is the same message you may get even if you typed in the URL correctly but the site you are trying to connect to is nonfunctional. It might mean that the server or computer to which you have connected is not working or is down for maintenance. Try again later if you're sure that you're typing in the correct URL.

If you consistently receive an error message for the same URL, it may indicate that the service is no longer available, or it has moved to another location. Unfortunately, sometimes Web sites disappear without leaving a trace or a forwarding address. In this case, your only option is to try going to some other home page for the information you want.
For example, let's say you want to go to the IBM home page to look for recent press releases that may affect your investment in the company's stock. To get there, you need to type "http://www.ibm.com" in the location box and press the **Enter** key. Now it's a question of exploring the page to see what it has to offer. A text link to another home page

appears in blue and is underlined, and a click on such a link takes you to a new location. You can also click on pictures and icons which are links to other home pages. Once you get the hang of it, exploring the Web can be a very exciting endeavor. You'll be able to follow links to Web sites all around the world, and you may be surprised at the information you'll be able to uncover in your cyber-travels.

SEARCH TOOLS

WebCrawler is the search engine that comes with the AOL Internet connection, but it never hurts to have a number of several other very good search tools you can use (and their URLs). Here's a list of search engines and their URLs:

Excite (http://www.excite.com)

Yahoo! (http://www.yahoo.com)

Lycos (http://www.lycos.com)

WebCrawler (http://www.webcrawler.com)

OpenText (http://www.opentext.com)

Infoseek NetSearch (http://www.infoseek.com)

Alta Vista (http://www.altavista.digital.com)

AOL'S FRIENDLY NEWSGROUPS

When it comes to newsgroups, AOL is as friendly as online services get; AOL translates the Internet name of a newsgroup into a more readily understandable name. For example, the Internet name for the Test Messages Go Here newsgroup is aol.newsgroups.test. Newsgroups on the Internet are organized into two general groups: main newsgroups and alternative newsgroups. You should know about these names if you're going to do a lot of exploring widely on the Internet and use the Expert Add feature that AOL offers (for which you need the entire Internet name). Using Expert Add is a way to add newsgroups to your list of favorite newsgroups.

Here's a list of some of the main and alternative group categories, their focus, and an example of each (in parentheses).

comp—Information about computers and computer science (artificial intelligence-comp.ai)

news—Information about news (administering news-news.adm)

rec—Information about recreation (football news-rec.sports.football)

sci—Information about science (astronomy-sci.astro)

soc—Information about the social sciences (history-soc.history)

talk—Forums on controversial topics (abortion-talk.abortion)

misc—Everything else! (taxes-misc.taxes)

How Do You Find a Home Page?

 This, of course, is the $64,000 question. There's no central listing of home pages, and since anyone can create one, literally thousands are being added to the Web each day. Even the URL used by a company one day could be changed to another URL the next.

There are several strategies you can take. You know that most URLs begin with http://www. Also, there are a number of common extensions used to identify the type of Web site you are entering. For example, ".com" stands for commercial, ".gov" stands for government, ".edu" stands for educational, and ".org" stands for other types of organizations. So many URLs for companies will take the form http://www.CompanyName.com, URLs for governmental agencies will take the form http://www.Agency.gov, and so forth. The URL for IBM, for example, would be http://www.IBM.com.

Sometimes the last character in an address is an additional forward slash (/).

If you don't know a URL, you might be able to guess. Here are some suggestions:

1. Take an educated guess, and enter the company or organization's name. If you want to find out what Mobil Oil has on its home page, try http://www.Mobil.com (it works). How about Microsoft? Try http://www.microsoft.com. You've already seen the URL for the SEC, which is http://www.sec.gov.

2. You can always call the company or organization to ask for its home page address or Web site address.

3. Talk with others who use AOL or other services to find out what the Web has to offer and what interesting home pages they have. The best way to learn about page addresses is by exploring the Web, talking with others, and using tools such as **URouLette** or search services like **Yahoo!**, **Excite**, **Alta Vista**, or **InfoSeek**.

URouLette is a home page address that acts like a roulette wheel. When you click on it, it takes you to another home page, but it determines the home page by searching a database of home pages and making the selection by chance. You never know where you'll be going! Perhaps you'll end up at Microsoft, but you also may end up learning about solar energy at Harvard University (http://www2/excite/SFU.ca/pgm.)

Here's the URL for URouLette:

http://www.uroulette.com

4. Take advantage of the **Favorite Places** option in the AOL browser. When you do find a place you like, click on the heart-shaped icon above the display area to add it to your favorite places list. You can then easily go back to that home page whenever you want.

Searching on the Web

 If you spend any time on the Web, you'll quickly realize that although all these home pages are linked, there's really no overriding organization to what the Web contains. And because of this, there's no table of contents or index to which you can refer to find what you want. You have to search. Some people find the searching part of the fun, since searching usually reveals things you wouldn't otherwise find or be exposed to.

On the other hand, searching does take time. And the less help you have, the more time it takes. When you are considering where to invest your money, you want to find everything you can, and time is at a premium.

Necessity certainly is the mother of invention, and in the short time that the Web has been around, several Web search tools have been developed. Most notably, **WebCrawler** is the one that is used by AOL. You enter a word or phrase that you want to search for, and WebCrawler searches through the contents of the home pages it has already indexed. WebCrawler then returns to you a list of possible sites that might match the words you entered. Obviously, the more specific the search terms, the higher the likelihood that you'll find the information you're looking for.

Using WebCrawler

 To use the WebCrawler, follow these steps:

1. Double-click on the **Search The Internet** option listed in the Resources column (this is on the Internet Connection menu.)

2. Then, either click on the large **WebCrawler**

HOW TO READ A STOCK CHART OR TABLE

To begin, find the symbol for the stock you want to track, such as MSFT for Microsoft. Both tables and charts express the daily price of a stock as three values: HI, LOW, and CLOSE. The HI value is the highest price that the stock traded at that day, the LOW is the lowest price it traded for the day, and the CLOSE is simply the price of the day's last recorded trade. A typical chart will display these same numbers as a bar with a line drawn across it. The top of the bar is the HI, the bottom is the LOW, and the line drawn across the bar is the CLOSE. Often, the historical price and volume information are shown. They can give you a good view of the past performance of the stock.

A stock table also usually shows the 52-WEEK HI and LOW price, which is a good indicator of a stock's recent volatility. The DIV is the dividend paid to stockholders by the company, expressed as the number of cents per share per quarter (if any). The price-to-earnings ratio (P/E) is widely used to measure the market's valuation of a stock, and expresses the current price per share divided by the current earnings per share. The VOL is the volume of shares (usually in thousands) traded on the exchange that day, and is a good indicator of the market's interest in a stock. If a stock's price drops quickly on high volume, it is typically an indicator that many people are selling the stock to get out of that investment. High volume and a rising price usually indicate that many people want to get in on an investment.

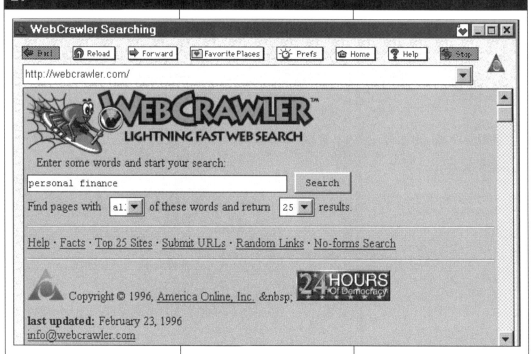

WebCrawler Searching

http://webcrawler.com/

WEBCRAWLER™
LIGHTNING FAST WEB SEARCH

Enter some words and start your search:

personal finance   Search

Find pages with [al:▼] of these words and return [25 ▼] results.

Help · Facts · Top 25 Sites · Submit URLs · Random Links · No-forms Search

Copyright © 1996, America Online, Inc.

last updated: February 23, 1996
info@webcrawler.com

icon, or double-click on the **Search the Web** item in the menu.

3. Enter the search words that describe what you want.

4. Click on **Search.** The WebCrawler will return the default of 25 responses ("hits"). For instance, asking WebCrawler to search "personal finance" will find over 2,000 documents! The word "investing" turns up over 1,500 documents.

Now you can go to any one of these locations (most are home pages) just by clicking on the underlined text.

Discovering Newsgroups

 You might read the newspaper regularly at home, but you're really in for a treat when you start working with newsgroups, also called **USENET news, Net News,** and **Internet News.** A newsgroup is like a big discussion group that focuses on a specific topic, such as football, physics, movies, pasta, and, of course, investments. In fact, there are over 30,000 such groups, so there's bound to be something for everyone.

The best thing about newsgroups is that you can easily jump into any of the ongoing discussions, ask questions, and offer com-

ments and feedback. It's as if you entered a room where many people are discussing the same topic, which in your case, might be the next quarterly report for IBM, whether that speculative penny-stock is really worth sinking your hard-earned cash into, or whether last year's top-performing mutual fund still looks good for the year ahead.

AOL Newsgroups

 Newsgroups are organized by general categories, such as business, social issues, humanities, and computers. The newsgroups that are available to you through AOL are those the AOL system administrator decides are useful and appropriate. So some will be accessible, while others you may find only outside of AOL via another news reader, such as **NewsXpress** or **Netscape.**

Most newsgroups are un-moderated, which means there's no one in charge of postings or to decide what's appropriate. As with most Internet activities, you own your own words. That is, no one but you is responsible for what is posted under your account.

When you use the **Add Newsgroups** button on the AOL Newsgroups screen, you will be able to select from the many newsgroups available through AOL. This feature maintains a large collection of newsgroups orga-nized on several dif-ferent levels in a hierarchical fashion. Here's what each level is called, with an example of what you might find at each level:

- **Categories** (such as Miscellaneous, Uncategorized Newsgroups)

- **Topics** (such as misc.invest)

- **Newsgroups** (such as Analyzing Market Trends with Technical Methods)

- **Subjects** (such as Investment Newsletters)

As you proceed through the hierarchy, the informa-tion becomes more specif-ic. You make your contri-bution to a newsgroup dis-cussion, called a "posting," at the Subject level.

Using AOL Newsgroups

 To begin using AOL Newsgroups, click on the **Newsgroups** icon on the Internet Connection menu,

or use the Keyword "Newsgroups." You'll see the Newsgroups opening screen, and you can elect to do one of several different things just by clicking on the appropriate icon:

1. Go immediately to the **Read My Newsgroups** icon for a short sample of newsgroups that AOL thinks you may have an interest in. It's a way of introducing you to some of what's available. Your person-al choices for news-groups will also be list-ed here. You can delete those newsgroups for which you don't want current information and add your own to

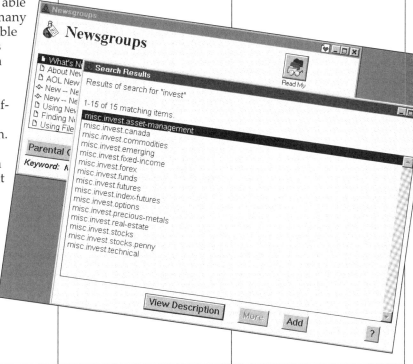

create a personalized list of only those newsgroups with which you want to keep up.

When you find a newsgroup you want to join, click on the **Add** button on AOL's newsgroups screen, and it will be added to your Read My Newsgroups list. Every time you open you'll have a nifty list of your favorite newsgroups.

2. Read newsgroup information offline (**Read Offline**). You will need to set up your FlashSessions options to download unread newsgroup messages by clicking on **Mail,** then **FlashSessions** from the AOL menu.

3. Add a newsgroup (**Add Newsgroups**) to the Read My

Newsgroups list, so each time you open the Newsgroups feature, AOL will be sure to update those categories.

4. Use **Expert Add** to add a newsgroup to your personal list if you know the full Internet name of the newsgroup.

5. Finally, **Search All Newsgroups** using a key term such as "Invest" to find those that might contain information you're interested in. If you want a description of a newsgroup, click on **View Description.** To add it to your personal list, click on **Add.**

Adding a Specific Newsgroup to Your Personal List

 AOL provides you with access to thousands of newsgroups. To examine what's available, click on the **Add Newsgroups** icon in the Newsgroups opening screen. You'll see a complete listing of newsgroup categories available to you. To add a specific newsgroup to your list of newsgroups, follow these steps:

1. Click on the category you want to explore, **Business and Commercial Newsgroups,** for example, to highlight it.

2. Click on **List Topics,** and you'll see a list of the newsgroups within topics.

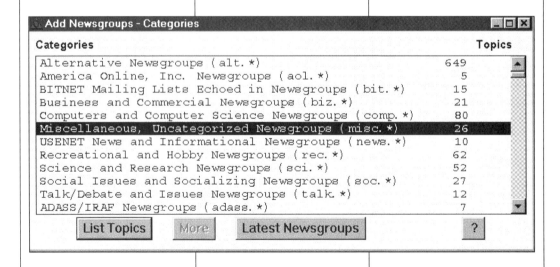

3. Click on the **List Newsgroups** button, and you'll see the subjects within the newsgroup.

4. If you want to add this newsgroup to your personal list, click on the **Add** button on the screen. You can also examine the contents of the newsgroup by double-clicking on the newsgroup's title.

Creating a Discussion Topic: Posting a Test Message

 Newsgroups can provide a wealth of information, but the real value is that you can read and contribute, which means posting messages. To practice posting, you can use a special newsgroup area named **Test Messages Go Here,** which AOL automatically lists in the Read My Newsgroups area.

Here's how to post a message to **Test Messages Go Here**:

1. In the Newsgroups window, click on the **Read My Newsgroups** icon.

2. Double-click on **Test Messages Go Here:** When you do this, you'll see a listing of the subjects in the Test Messages Go Here newsgroup.

3. Click on the **Send New Message** icon at the top of the screen. You'll see the **Post New Message** screen. You can also see the official Internet name of this newsgroup, which is aol.newsgroups-test.

4. Enter a subject and press **Tab** to move to the next field.

5. Enter your message and click on **Send.**

The message you sent should show up in the Subjects listing. It may take some time to work its way through the system, and first you'll have to close the window and reopen it (so it can be refreshed) before you see the actual subject.

That's how you create a subject to which people can make a contribution. But read on to learn how to make your own contribution.

Exploring and Contributing to a Newsgroup

 Do the following to read messages in any of the newsgroups:

1. Double-click on the subject line to see the contributions to the newsgroup.

2. Double-click on the message you want to read or respond to.

INDEXES: COMPARING PERFORMANCE

Simply put, indexes show the relative value of a group of similar investments over time and are used by investors to gauge the general performance of the market. Indexes are created and maintained by companies such as Dow Jones or Standard & Poor's, and offer investors methods to measure the performance of their investments. The Dow Jones Industrial Average, for example, is composed of a group of 30 of the largest and most influential corporations in America. The index is calculated daily by Dow Jones and is probably the most widely watched stock market index. Here are some of the other indexes that you might see:

- **Dow Jones Utility Average**

- **Dow Jones Transportation Average**

- **Standard & Poor's 500 Stock Index**

- **Index of Leading Economic Indicators**

- **Bond Buyer's Index**

- **Consumer Price Index**

- **Nasdaq Composite Index**

- **New York Stock Exchange Index**

- **Producer Price Index**

To learn more about these indexes, go to keyword "Company Research," then scroll down the list box and double-click on the Wall Street Words Dictionary. In the search area on the screen that appears, type the word "index" and click on the Look Up button.

To move around:

- The **Previous** button takes you to the previous message in the subject you've been exploring.

- The **Next** button takes you to the next message.

To make a contribution to the newsgroup:

- The **Reply to Group** button lets you post a message to the highlighted subject. Anything that's created and sent using this option can be read by anyone who reads this newsgroup. You make a contribution to the entire group.

- The **E-Mail to Author** button allows you to send a private message via AOL e-mail to the author of the message.

Using Gophers

 A Gopher is an Internet utility that allows you to search through thousands of Internet sites and databases by pointing and clicking on a series of menus.

To use the Gopher feature, follow these steps:

1. Click on the **Gopher & WAIS** icon on the Internet Connection screen. You'll be taken to the main Gopher screen. WAIS stands for Wide Area Information Server. Like the WebCrawler, it searches through databases and returns information from a specified content area.

2. Double-click on the category you want to explore. Then select the actual Gopher site you want to visit.

Where Is That Site?

 If, for some reason, you can't find what you want in any of the main group listings, click on the **Search** icon on the main Gopher screen. You'll see a prompt, which asks you to enter a subject.

For example, enter the word "bonds" and see how many matching entries you find. The list is not organized in any particular fashion, and you are on your own to explore those that you think may be valuable.

The fascinating thing about searching through thousands of Gopher sites using a search term is that you never know what you'll find. The search may return a lot of unusable material, but it may yield exactly the information you need.

Gopher Treasures

 In an effort to help you reduce the amount of time you may spend burrowing down some dead-end Gopher holes, AOL created the **Gopher Treasures** area.

Gopher Treasures is a collection of some of the most interesting Gopher sites on the Net. Topics range from "A Timeline of the Counter-Culture" to "C-SPAN" and the "Glasgow Golf Gopher." The collection is a terrific place to get started when you're exploring the gopher utility. You never know what's in Gopher Treasures. It's a matter of stopping by every now and then and examining the Gopher sites that are listed.

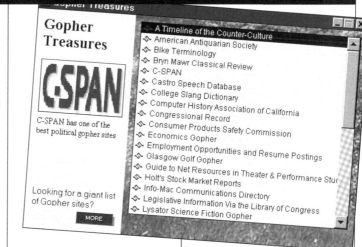

Gopher Treasures

C-SPAN has one of the best political gopher sites

Looking for a giant list of Gopher sites?

MORE

A Timeline of the Counter-Culture
- American Antiquarian Society
- Bike Terminology
- Bryn Mawr Classical Review
- C-SPAN
- Castro Speech Database
- College Slang Dictionary
- Computer History Association of California
- Congressional Record
- Consumer Products Safety Commission
- Economics Gopher
- Employment Opportunities and Resume Postings
- Glasgow Golf Gopher
- Guide to Net Resources in Theater & Performance Stud
- Holt's Stock Market Reports
- Info-Mac Communications Directory
- Legislative Information Via the Library of Congress
- Lysator Science Fiction Gopher

Using FTP

 Okay, you've found the information you're looking for. Now what? **FTP,** or File Transfer Protocol, is the tool you use to exchange files with other Internet sites. For example, you might learn of a site that has documents with information for investors, and you may want to download a file, examine it, and pursue any opportunities that might seem interesting. There are two ways to use the FTP feature: You can examine favorite sites (picked by AOL), or you can search for another site.

To examine favorite sites, follow these steps:

1. Click on the **FTP** icon on the opening Internet screen.

2. Click on the **Go to FTP** icon on the File Transfer Protocol (FTP) screen.

INVESTMENT SITES FOR KIDS

Want to teach your children about the value of a dollar and how to make their money grow? You can send them to AOL's KidzBiz site to learn about many aspects of business and investing. Press CTRL-K to get to the keyword screen, then type "KidzBiz" and click on GO. KidzBiz offers your kids a fun way to explore all sorts of investment-related information, find other kids who want to trade stuff, and learn about the value of their money. From the KidzBiz main screen, click on the Mind Your Dollars icon, and you'll get right to the Mind Your Dollars screen. The features offered here include:

Trading Desk—A place for kids to trade with other kids.

Chore Exchange—This is a place where kids can look up what chores other kids have to do, and how much compensation they get (really!).

Street Cents—Something like *Consumer Reports* for kids. Offers the lowdown on the best products and values.

Money Matters—Articles and advice for kids about how to manage their money. Great stuff here!

The Stock Market—Explains how the market is run and how to join the Stock Market Game, a national game run by the Securities Industry Foundation for Economic Education. Schools sign up teams of students, who are given an imaginary $100,000 to invest in a portfolio of their own choosing.

You'll see a listing of FTP sites; these are some of the most frequented sites for downloading files. You can then click on any one of the sites and begin exploring. If you want to explore a site that is not listed, then click on **Other Site.**

For example, if you connect to the AOL FTP site (by double-clicking on **ftp.aol.com**), you'll find a listing of directories and files. Since you probably have no idea what's contained in them, it's best to first read any welcoming files, usually named something like "Welcome" or "Read Me."

FTP sites are not particularly user-friendly, and the best way to approach them is to know what you're looking for. Even if you just go exploring, you're likely to find additional directories and files that are poorly described, cryptically named, and mysterious.

The best way to use FTP is to know where you're going in the first place. For example, if you want a giant list of listserve groups, an FTP site that contains this information is InfoServices, at ftp://ftp.nic.surfnet.nl/surfnet/net-management/earn/services/listserv.lists/, a software repository that maintains a huge number

of listserve groups, as well as a tremendous amount of other information. You can use AOL to download from them, or you can enter the above address (yes, the whole thing!) into AOL's Keyword entry screen (remember, **CTRL-K** for short).

Searching for Good FTP Sites

 FTP is not commonly used in the world of investments and finance. This is especially true for novices since you have to rely on some knowledge of what files are stored at which sites if you want to make good use of the utility. Most investment information is now available on the World Wide Web, and you will probably spend most of your energy and surfing time there.

However, AOL does offer the **Search for FTP Sites** icon on the main FTP screen. When you click on this icon, you'll be prompted to provide words that describe what you're looking for. What AOL returns is a list of FTP sites that might contain the information you need.

The only way to find out whether or not that's the information you need is to actually download from the site and explore. If you

File Transfer Protocol - FTP

File Transfer Protocol (FTP) is a way to access the vast file resources of the Internet. The files and archives you can reach by FTP are maintained by organizations outside America Online FTP Sites -- locations containing file archives -- are often run by volunteers or non-profit organizations. You will have better luck connecting to their sites during off-peak hours, 7 PM to 6 AM local time. They'll appreciate it too!

Search for FTP Sites

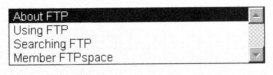

About FTP
Using FTP
Searching FTP
Member FTPspace

Go To FTP

Keyword: FTP

can find an e-mail address associated with the site, write to that address and ask if there's a file explaining what the contents of the FTP site are, and whether it can be accessed through the FTP tool or sent to you.

INVESTING ONLINE
WITH AOL

NOW THAT
YOU'VE BEEN
INTRODUCED TO
THE BASICS

on how to use AOL and the Internet, it's time to dig in to the resources available for investors on America Online. You could, of course, simply start with a Keyword search on words such as "Finance" or "Investments." A search on Keyword "Finance" returns over 50 topics ranging from taxes to entrepreneurship to parenting to horoscopes!

Some of the results may be exactly what you are looking for, while others may have only a slight relevance to topics of interest. For example, the "Horoscopes" entry will likely have some information about your current or future financial situation. But maybe you're looking for something a little more concrete in your quest for advice or information on your investments!

Getting Stock Quotes and Company Data

 One of the primary tools for investors is the ticker, and AOL offers the **Quotes and Portfolios** screen so you can get quotes and charts for various stocks quickly.

You can also use this feature to look up a company's ticker symbol if you don't know it. Quotes are delayed by 15 minutes, so if you need real-time access to the ongoing trading activities of the major exchanges, you will need to find another, probably much more expensive, service.

For most people, a delay of 15 minutes is not a problem. This usually provides plenty of information to keep track of the market's progress (and sometimes too much!). It rarely pays to watch the little up and down ticks during the course of a single day unless your primary inter-

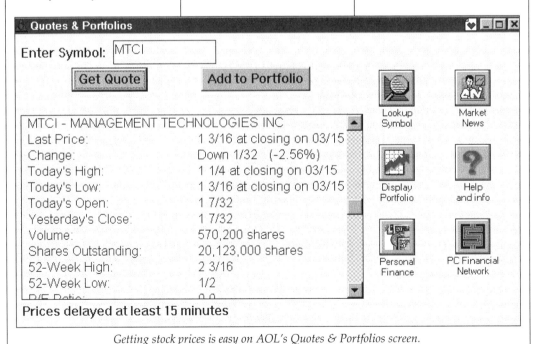

Getting stock prices is easy on AOL's Quotes & Portfolios screen.

est is day trading for small, short-term gains).

To get to the **Stock Quote** screen, use the Keyword "Quotes." Then click on the **Lookup** button to quickly look up a ticker symbol for just about any company that trades on the major stock exchanges, such as NYSE, Nasdaq, and AMEX.

If you are interested in perusing graphs of a stock's performance over time, or if you'd like to get a listing of historical High Low Close prices and volumes for a particular stock, you can use the Keyword "Historical Quotes." This will take you to a screen on which you can view charts and historical price/performance information for stocks.

You can set the time period for viewing the information either by using one of the default options, or by clicking on the **Custom** option and setting your own time period for the historical data. The **Preferences** button allows you to customize your graphs by setting the display options, including whether or not to show the day's trading volume, a 50-day moving average of the stock price, or the stock's relative strength in comparison to market aver-

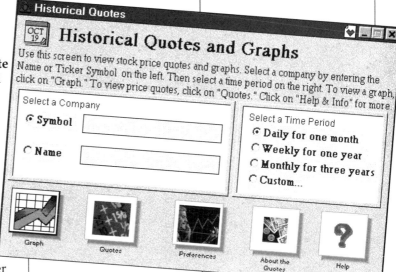

ages. You can also set download options so you can download historical stock data in plain comma-delimited format or in a format that can be used by Quicken or MetaStock.

Market News

 Further information about the recent activities of the market is available by clicking on the **Market News** icon to get to the **Stock Market Details**

screen. (You can also get to Stock Market Details by using the Keyword "Market News.") From here, you can get up-to-date news on the markets and keep track of the various indexes used to track the market's performance. You can also search the news for topics of interest, find Moody's and Standard & Poor's ratings for stocks and mutual funds, and get a listing of top Internet sites for investors.

The **Stock Market Details** area groups economic and financial information by categories that you can select by clicking on the drop-down category list to the left of the text that says, "Click at left for more categories." Currently, there are five separate categories in which AOL stores market information, and each of these has numerous subcategories. Here are the main categories, and just a few of the subcategories that you can explore:

Commodities

- Daily commodity summary
- Grains, oilseeds, and meals
- Livestock
- Metals
- World oil prices

Economic Indicators

- U.S. construction spending
- U.S. consumer confidence
- U.S. factory orders
- U.S. gross domestic product
- U.S. housing starts

- U.S. weekly jobless claims

International Markets

- China stock report
- Czech stock report
- International market rundown

Money & Currency

- Hourly currency cross-rates
- Hourly foreign exchange rates
- U.S. money funds
- U.S. treasuries focus

Stock Market Details

- Markets at a glance

CAVEAT EMPTOR: EVERYONE HAS OPINIONS ABOUT WHAT'S HOT!

The ongoing discussions on the message boards can be a good source of information, but they can also very easily degenerate into online shouting matches and cheerleading sessions for people who have had the good fortune to be positioned in "winning" stocks. "Let the buyer beware" is probably the best advice anyone can give regarding the information that is posted on these discussion boards. A considerable amount of hype is generated by people attempting to manipulate the prices of various stocks, and there have been plenty of instances in which stock prices

have experienced short-term jumps because of hype only to drop back later when the original "promoters" of the stock sell their holdings at a profit and leave everyone else holding the bag.

The primary problem with message board discussions (and this applies equally to Usenet newsgroups) is that you can never be sure about the identity or the intentions of the various people posting information. The anonymity of people on message boards can be both a blessing and a curse. If you want to protect your privacy, it is certainly advantageous to be able to post messages and ask questions by using a screen name or alias. However, people who intentionally post incorrect or misleading information are also left unaccountable for the consequences of their actions.

Certainly not everyone touting an investment is a hypester or snake-oil salesperson. There are probably more genuinely honest people posting messages than charlatans. But even well-intentioned messages can be misleading. Anyone who makes an investment is likely to have a positive point of view about it, even if everyone else thinks it is a waste of money. People driven by hope often see great potential in the smallest things, and their messages will most often reflect their unbridled optimism, even if it isn't warranted.

On the flip side, there are plenty of folks who will talk down an investment because they missed out on the best opportunities to buy in, or because they are "shorting" a stock. When you invest in a short position on a stock, you are essen-

- Stock brief open/mid-day/close

- Nasdaq most active

- NYSE, AMEX largest changes

- NYSE closing averages

Business News

 The **Business News** icon on Market News takes you to a screen where you can read top business headlines for the day from numerous investment publications. This screen is similar to the Market News screen in that it, too, groups information by categories that are accessible

by clicking on the drop-down list box, to the left of the text that says, "Click at left for more categories." You can get directly to the Business News screen by using the Keyword

"Business News" from anywhere in AOL. Here is a list of the primary categories and a few subcategories:

---

tially betting that the stock price will drop rather than increase. People who bet "short" will get very uncomfortable when the stock's price rises, just as people who bet "long" (bought shares expecting the price to rise) get very nervous when the price drops. Nervous people often post "gloom and doom" messages because it is never a pleasant feeling to watch your investment returns go negative. You can never be quite sure of other people's motivations, so you can't tell if the information they present is accurate.

The primary point is simply this: Never invest in anything without doing your homework first! This means finding out the facts by using the various services on AOL and the Internet that offer real, solid information on a company's

history, its projected growth rates, and the risks involved with investing in that company. If you are unable to find any information on an investment, chances are that it is a high-risk proposition.

Of course, new companies that haven't developed any kind of track record may not have much information available out there, and it would be a shame to miss out on a good opportunity simply because the company didn't have a history. But you can always contact a company directly! Request an investor's kit, which usually has financial information, product information, and expectations for the company's future. While the company will most certainly be biased in terms of its future prospects, the financial data should be accurate and will give you a good sense of the

stability and strength of the company.

Keep the word "risk" at the forefront of your thoughts any time you intend to invest your hard-earned money. While it is true that people have doubled and tripled their investments, or even had ten or twentyfold returns on some investments, it is equally true that people have lost every penny on risky investments that went south. You should definitely understand and accept the risks inherent in investing before throwing your money into the great sea of opportunities out there.

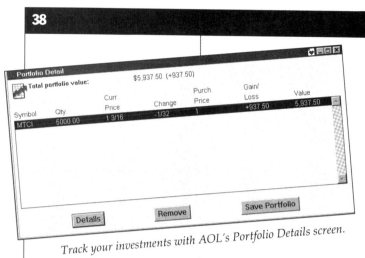

Track your investments with AOL's Portfolio Details screen.

UNDERSTANDING MUTUAL FUNDS

A mutual fund enables you to invest in a diversified portfolio of stocks, bonds, and other investment options, thereby minimizing some of the risks involved. Mutual funds are managed by professional investors who attempt to maximize the gains made by the fund, while managing the risk for you. There are mutual funds designed to invest in particular industry groups, such as high-tech or biotech (called sector funds), or to fulfill specific investment objectives, such as preservation of capital, capital growth, or aggressive growth. There are literally thousands of mutual funds available today, so you should try to decide what types of investments you are interested in, and then look for funds that have good historical performance and returns. Make sure to research any fund before you invest, and remember that just because a fund is managed by a professional, you are not necessarily completely protected from losses. Any investment involves risk, and the more aggressive the objectives of the fund, the more risky the investment.

Top Business

- Various news articles and stories

Industry News

- Government & business
- Company actions
- Company changes
- Automobiles
- Biotechnology

International Business

- Various folders listed by country or region

Additional Resources

- *The New York Times* business section
- Mercury Center business section
- American Yellow Pages
- The Nightly Business Report

You can search news from this screen, and you can get to other areas on AOL such as the **Company Research** area where you can find detailed informa-

tion about specific companies. You can also click on **Top Internet Sites** for useful investment sites.

As you continue to move along through the various services that AOL has to offer investors, you'll find a great deal of overlap in the links that take you from one place to another. This is a wonderful convenience when you start digging in because you won't have to get back to particular screens to find what you are looking for. You can explore this maze with impunity. No matter how deeply you dig, you'll probably wind up right back where you started, but with a lot more knowledge to your credit!

Keeping Track of Your Portfolio

 AOL offers a terrific feature for regular investors in its **Portfolio Detail** area. There you can build your own portfolio then add to it from the **Quotes and Portfolios** screen. Simply click on the **Add to Portfolio.** The system will ask you to enter your purchase price and number of shares. Then it will save this information for later reference.

To get back to your own portfolio later, use the keyword "Portfolio." AOL

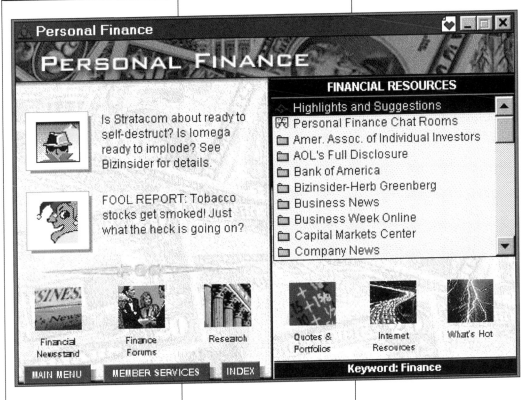

will automatically calculate the current value of your portfolio based on the market price of your shares.

AOL Financial Services

 The best place to begin your online investment education might be the AOL **Personal Finance** center.

Ironically, when you search on the Keywords "Finance" or "Investments," this area is not among the results listed! But it contains valuable links to other finance and investment forums, so make sure you know how to find it. It may turn out to be your financial headquarters on AOL. To get there, use the Keyword "Finance," but instead of clicking on **Search,** click on **Go.**

Some of the links you'll see are:

- The Financial Newsstand
- Company News
- Company Research
- Message Boards
- Chat Rooms

The Financial Newsstand

 When you click on the **Financial Newsstand** icon on the Personal Finance screen, you'll be transported to an area of AOL where you can find just about any financial news you may be searching for. You can also get here by using the Keyword "Financial News."

Many local, national, and international publications are accessible from here by simply clicking on an icon or double-clicking on a folder. In addition to providing links to news and

Keyword: Financial News

information sites on AOL, this area also contains links to FTP, Gopher, and World Wide Web sites.

One of the great benefits of AOL is that it is very well integrated with the Internet, and sometimes it becomes difficult to distinguish between the proprietary services on AOL and the many Internet sites and services that are out there. Some of the news services available on the Financial Newsstand are:

- *Business Week*
- *Investor's Business Daily*
- *The New York Times* business section
- *The Chicago Tribune*
- *Holt's Market Report* (on the Net)

- *Inc. Magazine*
- *San Jose Mercury News* business section

Each of these publications provides a different perspective on the world of business, finance, and investments. For example, *Investor's Business Daily* focuses on how news and developments in the busi-

ness world specifically affect investors, billing itself as "The Newspaper for Important Decision Makers." (Certainly when it comes to making your own investment decisions, no one is as important as you!)

Inc. Magazine, on the other hand, takes the perspective of the business owner, and provides a great deal of information for entrepreneurs, as well as up-close and personal looks at new and growing companies. This might be a great place to find out about relatively young companies that are looking forward to very bright and successful futures, the kinds that investors love to hear about!

The *San Jose Mercury News* business section has a decided bent toward Silicon Valley (high-tech)

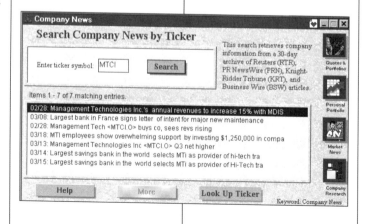

Keyword: Company News

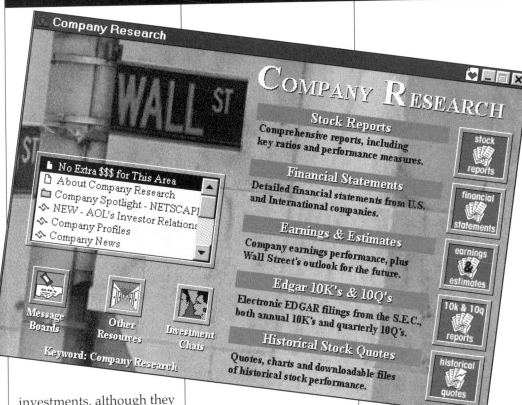

investments, although they have plenty of other investment information available as well.

Company News

 One item in the list of connections available from the Financial Newsstand that you will most certainly use repeatedly is the Company News selection. If you double-click on the **Company News** folder, AOL will display a search screen that allows you to search a database for news from a 30-day archive of articles from the following news services:

- Reuters
- PR NewsWire
- *Knight-Ridder Tribune*
- Business Wire

This search capability comes in very handy when you are trying to keep track of particular companies and any news or press releases that may affect the price of that company's stock. When you enter a ticker in the search box and click on **Search,** AOL will return a list of articles. To read one, just double-click on the article you want in the list of available stories. And from here, like many of the screens in AOL, you can get to other locations of interest to investors. Icons for **Quotes & Portfolios,** your **Personal Portfolio** (Portfolio Detail), **Market News,** and **Company Research** are all available from this screen, so you can dig even deeper into the treasures available online. You can also look up a ticker symbol from this screen, in case you've forgotten the symbol of the stock you want to search the news for.

Company Research

 To get more in-depth coverage of particular investments, you'll want to visit the **Company Research** forum by using the Keyword "Company Research."

For example, you can get stock reports (provided by Morningstar Investor

REAL ESTATE RESOURCES

While most people think of stocks or mutual funds when they discuss investing, many others think of real estate. Historically, real estate has been one of the most stable and reliable investments available. AOL offers the Real Estate Selections center, which contains a good collection of information for real estate investors and homebuyers. This site is accessible by using the keyword "Real Estate," and it contains the following hotlink buttons:

• **Real Estate Center**

• *Home* magazine

• **Homeowners Forum**

• **MixStar (mortgage prospects)**

• **Real Estate Web Sites**

• **Real Estate Xtra**

• **Homes & Land Online**

Whether you're interested in real estate as an investment or are looking for a home, the AOL's Real Estate Selections area gets you off to a good start.

Services) on numerous companies, which include historical performance data, a summary of the company's business operations, as well as comparisons with other companies in the same industry, and important ratios such as the price-earnings (PE) ratio, the price-book ratio, and so on. Also available is a breakdown of the company's current and historical financial position, the dividend history of the stock, and recent balance sheets.

The **Stock Reports** area also includes a stock screening service provided by the American Association of Individual Investors (AAII). This service allows you to search or "screen" for stocks that fit certain criteria, such as

low PE ratios, high or low earnings surprises from quarterly reports, dividend income, and others.

The stock screen is a great way to discover stocks that fit your particular investment objectives without having to pore over thousands of research reports. Of course, Morningstar also provides useful general information, such as **Basics of Investing, Stock Selection,** and the **Reference Shelf.** Valuable data is available for both the expert and the novice investor.

From the Company Research screen, you can also get financial statements from Disclosure, Inc. This service provides you with balance sheets,

Access FirstCall's Earnings & Estimates screen from the Company Research screen.

Company Research Message Boards

Stock Message Boards
- Stock Market
- Stocks A
- Stocks B
- Stocks C
- Stocks D-E
- Stocks F-G
- Stocks H-J

Here he is ...BOB BEATY!
Why is it only rich people seem to make big money? Fortunately for the rest of us, there's "According to Bob..."

Herb Greenberg's Bizinsider!
They love and hate him. But they read him. Check out the Bizinsider message boards!

Company Research Message Boards
- Company Research Board
- Disclosure Document Board
- First Call Earnings Board
- Morningstar Equities Board
- Prophet (Hist. Quotes) Board

Other Investment Message Boards
- Business Week Message Boards
- Decision Point Message Boards
- Investor's Business Daily Message Boards
- Motley Fool Message Boards
- Nightly Business Report Message Boards

Company Research

income statements, and cash flow statements from over 22,000 United States and international companies. In addition, this area provides a great deal of general information for the investor, such as the **Wall Street Words Dictionary,** information about the Securities and Exchange Commission (SEC), and a brief overview of the various Securities acts that the U.S. government has instituted over the years to oversee the markets.

FirstCall, Inc. provides a link from the Company Research screen to their **Earnings Estimates** forum. This area is a great place to find out about projected earnings for thousands of companies. From the Earnings Estimates screen, simply click on the **Search Earnings & Estimates** bar, and you'll be presented with a text entry screen that will allow you to enter a ticker symbol or company name for which you want to find earnings estimates. If you click on the **View Noteworthy Stocks** bar, FirstCall will provide you with lists of stocks that meet certain criteria, very much like the stock screens provided by Morningstar on the Stock Reports screen.

The Noteworthy Stocks section includes lists such as "Upcoming Stock Splits & Dividends" for individual stocks, "Index Estimate Trends" for tracking trends in various market indexes, two "Surprise!" folders, which keep track of stocks that have either exceeded or not met earnings expectations, and the "Hot or Not?" folders, which offer opinions on various stocks.

Finally, the Company Research screen also provides a direct link to the SEC's **Edgar** database of corporate 10-Q and 10-K filings (provided by Disclosure, Inc.). Registered companies are required to file these reports with the SEC on a regular basis.

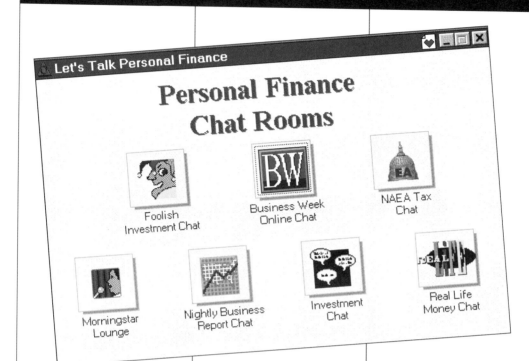

Personal Finance Chat Rooms

Foolish Investment Chat

Business Week Online Chat

NAEA Tax Chat

Morningstar Lounge

Nightly Business Report Chat

Investment Chat

Real Life Money Chat

MAKE TIME TO CHAT

Chat rooms are great places to exchange ideas or to ask questions of other investors online, in real time. Although some chat rooms seem to be open all the time, many organizations schedule chat room hours, such as:

- *BusinessWeek* Sunday Night Chat: Sundays at 9:00 p.m. Eastern Time, at the Business Week forum.

- Monday Night Tax Chats: Mondays from 9:00 p.m. to 11:00 p.m. Eastern Time, sponsored by the NAEA Tax Channel.

- Taxes and Investing 101: Mondays at 9:00 p.m. Eastern Time in Chat Room II of the Real Life Money Chat center.

- Your Money Matters: Tuesday from 8:00 p.m. to 10:00 p.m. at the Real Life Money Chat center.

The 10-K report provides a comprehensive, annual overview of the company, including financials, balance sheets, information about the industry sector in which the company participates, and a detailed management discussion of expectations about the company's future business prospects. The 10-Q report provides a similar overview of the company's progress, but it is filed on a quarterly rather than annual basis.

If you are really looking for the most accurate information possible, the SEC is likely to be the place. The SEC is, in a sense, the "stock market police" in

that they monitor the markets and keep track of corporate information. This regulatory body is charged with the responsibility for making sure that investors are not led astray by false claims or other investment scams. The information kept on file with the SEC will almost certainly be accurate and reliable, and this is a good place to get "inside information" about the performance of a particular company.

Of course, the Company Research screen provides links to other important financial resources on AOL, such as the **Historical Quotes** and **Company News** areas. One particularly interesting link from this screen is available by clicking on the **Message Boards** icon.

Message Boards

 Message boards are something like electronic corkboards where people can post messages that are available for everyone to see. The message boards on AOL are functionally very similar to the Usenet newsgroups of the Internet. The primary difference, of course, is that the AOL message boards are available only to members of the AOL service whereas Usenet is available to everyone on the Internet.

The Company Research Message Boards screen gives you access to many different groups of message sets that are maintained by various service providers on AOL. For example, *BusinessWeek* and *Investor's Business Daily* both maintain message boards. The Motley Fool service, which will be covered in greater depth later, offers one of the most popular and interesting groups of message boards on AOL.

There are specific message boards dedicated to company research, disclosure documents, FirstCall earnings, and Morningstar equities. And Prophet

Information Services, Inc., a company that specializes in providing historical data on companies, runs the Prophet board, which is accessible by using the Keyword "Prophet."

Personal Finance Chat Rooms

 If you want to discuss investment topics with people in a way that is more direct than on the investment message boards, you can participate in live online discussions in AOL's Personal Finance Chat Rooms.

There you can read messages as they are posted by individuals who are currently online. Then you can add your own remarks to the discussion, ask questions of knowledgeable individuals, or just sit back

and watch the flow of the "conversation." You can get to this screen by clicking on the Investment Chats icon on the Company Research screen (Keyword: "Company Research"). The Personal Finance Chat Rooms screen allows you to access the following discussions from one central location:

- Foolish Investment Chat (run by the Motley Fools)
- BusinessWeek Online Chat
- NAEA Tax Chat
- Morningstar Lounge
- Nightly Business Report Chat
- Investment Chat
- Real Life Money Chat

The same caveats that apply to the message boards also apply to the

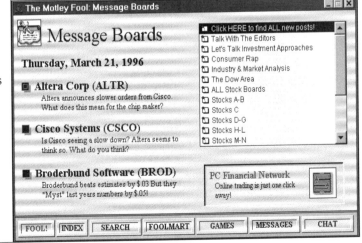

The American Association of Individual Investors

AAII Online

The American
of Individual Investors

- About AAII Online
- New Articles in AAII Online
- Financial/Retirement Planning
- Mutual Funds
- Stock Selection
- Managing Your Portfolio
- Dealing with Your Broker
- Computerized Investing
- Interviews with Fund Managers
- Bonds and Fixed Income Investments
- International Investing

Software Library

Need help tracking your investments, picking a stock, or buying new software. Look for help here.

Reference Library

Check inside to see the latest updates on discount brokers, dividend reinvestment plans, & member surveys.

Message Board   AAII Store   Search AAII Articles   Ask AAII   Calendar of Events

live discussions. Be careful with the information you receive, unless you're sure that it comes from a reputable and reliable source. Most of these chat rooms have regularly scheduled discussions that are moderated or hosted by reputable industry experts. It can be very enlightening to participate in these discussions because frequently you can get answers to important questions right from the source. Again, you are ultimately responsible for any investment decisions you make.

The American Association of Individual Investors

 The American Association of Individual Investors (AAII) is an independent, nonprofit organization that is dedicated to providing information and resources to individual investors. Its stated mission is "to assist individuals in becoming effective managers of their own investments."

In order to accomplish this goal, the AAII offers seminars and produces numer-

ous publications, educational videos, and other media-based educational tools for individual investors. It also registers members at local chapters in many cities. Membership benefits include discounted prices on educational items and seminars, as well as a regular newsletter with tips and information for investors.

The AAII maintains a forum where any AOL member can get access to a tremendous amount of detailed and interesting investment information. You can get here directly

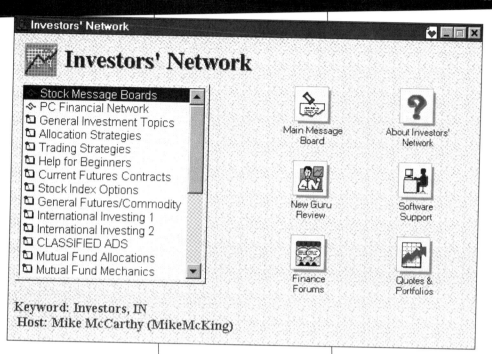

Investors' Network

Stock Message Boards
- PC Financial Network
- General Investment Topics
- Allocation Strategies
- Trading Strategies
- Help for Beginners
- Current Futures Contracts
- Stock Index Options
- General Futures/Commodity
- International Investing 1
- International Investing 2
- CLASSIFIED ADS
- Mutual Fund Allocations
- Mutual Fund Mechanics

Main Message Board

About Investors' Network

New Guru Review

Software Support

Finance Forums

Quotes & Portfolios

Keyword: Investors, IN
Host: Mike McCarthy (MikeMcKing)

by using the Keyword "AAII." Some of the folders on the AAII forum include

- Financial/Retirement Planning
- Mutual Funds
- Stock Selection
- Managing Your Portfolio
- Dealing with Your Broker
- Computerized Investing
- Interviews with Fund Managers

The AAII also maintains a message board for discussions, and a software library where you can download any number of excellent investment-related software products

such as charting and technical-analysis tools. This forum is a great place for both novice and experienced investors to get helpful information about investing.

The Investor's Network

 Another forum that can serve as a starting point for further exploration is the **Investor's Network.** To get here, use the Keyword "Investors." This forum provides a number of resources of general interest to investors, including a number of discussions on more esoteric topics such as futures and options. Here are some of the areas available on the Investor's Network:

- General Investment Topics
- Help for Beginners
- Trading Strategies
- General Futures/Commodities
- International Investing

This forum also has its own main message board, a software support area where you can download or get help with a number of investment-related software products, and the **New Guru Review** message board where "experts" post information on hot trends and you can post your replies and opinions.

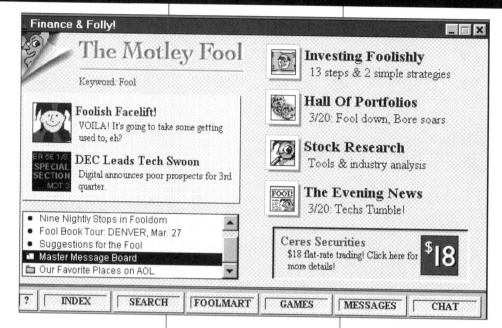

Finance & Folly!

The Motley Fool

Keyword: Fool

Foolish Facelift!
VOILA! It's going to take some getting used to, eh?

DEC Leads Tech Swoon
Digital announces poor prospects for 3rd quarter.

Investing Foolishly
13 steps & 2 simple strategies

Hall Of Portfolios
3/20: Fool down, Bore soars

Stock Research
Tools & industry analysis

The Evening News
3/20: Techs Tumble!

- Nine Nightly Stops in Fooldom
- Fool Book Tour: DENVER, Mar. 27
- Suggestions for the Fool
- Master Message Board
- Our Favorite Places on AOL

Ceres Securities
$18 flat-rate trading! Click here for more details!
$18

? | INDEX | SEARCH | FOOLMART | GAMES | MESSAGES | CHAT

The host of the Investor's Network, Mike McCarthy, is very helpful with answers to your investment and forum-related questions. This is a good place to learn about a wide variety of investments, especially if you are in unfamiliar territory.

The Motley Fool

 The Motley Fool area is actually a series of forums that cover the gamut of investment opportunities. The Fool is hosted by David and Tom Gardner, a couple of offbeat, very knowledgeable, and generally optimistic self-proclaimed "Fools." Their service is managed with a single, very important premise in mind: The

"Foolish" (yes, that's a capital F) individual investor who does homework can outperform the "Wise" investment professionals of Wall Street.

In their kingdom, the "Fool" is actually wise, and the "Wise" are actually fools. Huh? Yes, you got it right. It is a topsy-turvy world, but it is a wonderful place where you can get together with other Fools to discuss investments of all sorts. The Keyword to get here, of course, is "Fool"!

The Fools have established a complete online school of investing for those of us who need an education in the fine art of investing. **The Fool's School** is a

place where you can learn everything from the basics of investing to the intricate details of the "Dow Dividend Approach," an investment strategy used by the Fools to select a portfolio of stocks to (hopefully!) outperform the market averages. The School maintains a large collection of documents that you can read at your leisure to learn about almost any topic related to investing. The Fools also maintain a "model portfolio" of stocks that they've chosen. Their approach seems to be working: The return on their portfolio over the past year was over 100 percent!

If you're into the discussions on message boards, the Fools have also set up

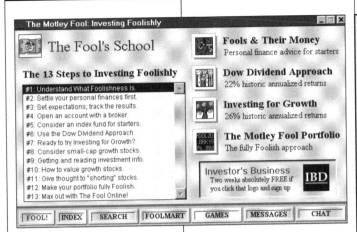

The Motley Fool: Investing Foolishly

The Fool's School

The 13 Steps to Investing Foolishly

#1: Understand What Foolishness Is.
#2: Settle your personal finances first.
#3: Set expectations; track the results.
#4: Open an account with a broker.
#5: Consider an index fund for starters.
#6: Use the Dow Dividend Approach.
#7: Ready to try Investing for Growth?
#8: Consider small-cap growth stocks.
#9: Getting and reading investment info.
#10: How to value growth stocks.
#11: Give thought to "shorting" stocks.
#12: Make your portfolio fully Foolish.
#13: Max out with The Fool Online!

Fools & Their Money
Personal finance advice for starters

Dow Dividend Approach
22% historic annualized returns

Investing for Growth
26% historic annualized returns

The Motley Fool Portfolio
The fully Foolish approach

Investor's Business
Two weeks absolutely FREE if
you click that logo and sign up   IBD

FOOL!   INDEX   SEARCH   FOOLMART   GAMES   MESSAGES   CHAT

their own series of boards for discussing a wide variety of topics, ranging from individual stocks to investment approaches to industry and market analysis. These boards are similar to the message boards on other forums, but the Fools' philosophy tends to influence the tone of postings, for better or worse. Don't forget to do your own research before making any investment decisions! The Foolish message boards, although generally guided by Foolish principles, can degenerate as easily as any of the other message boards online.

The Motley Fool forums are well run and well organized. You can hang out here with people of like mind and gather a tremendous amount of useful investment information. The screens are nicely designed, with a row of

buttons at the bottom of each one that allow you to find quickly other sections that may be of interest to you.

Click on the **Index** button to get an alphabetized list of areas available in the Fool forums, as well as areas that are of general interest to investors, such as the SEC and the Evening News. The Index contains enough to keep you exploring for days on end, and there's no doubt that you'll run into something informative, interesting, and fun while digging through the Fools' offerings.

If you want to find something specific in the Foolish forums, you can click on the **Search** button and enter a topic you are interested in. The Fools search screen allows you to search a variety of sources

THE SOFTWARE LIBRARY

AOL offers a comprehensive software library where you can search for and download all sorts of software, from games to investment-related programs that help you manage your money. To get to the AOL software library, press CTRL-K to get to your keyword screen, then type "Software Library" and click on GO.

If you want to find investment-related software, click on the File Search icon on the Software Library screen, then enter the word "Invest" or "Investments." The software library contains hundreds of files that will help you track your portfolio, create stock charts, and use technical analysis to try to project stock price movements. Below are a few of the programs that are available:

• Investment Tracker

• Financial Calculator

• Rent Manager

• Wall Street Simulator

• Chart Generator

Most of the programs available are offered as shareware, which means that you can evaluate the program free for a limited time. If you decide that you like the software and want to continue using it, you'll need to purchase (or register) the software directly with the author. Most programs come with a README.TXT or similar file that tells you how to register.

for information on particular investments, including:

- Stock Reports
- Earnings and Estimates
- Company News
- Financial Statements
- 10-K and 10-Q reports
- Historical Quotes

The Fools also offer an online store where you can order all sorts of stuff. You can sign up for e-mail delivery of numerous financial and news reports, and you can order books or research reports that will prove to be very helpful in your ongoing investor's education. Of course, the Fools would be happy to sell you any number of other miscellaneous items; you can order Foolish T-shirts, Foolish boxer shorts (no kidding!), Foolish mouse pads, Foolish golf equipment, Foolish caps—the list goes on! If you're into wearing items decorated with little Foolish characters and the word "fool" in various places, this is the store for you!

The Fools maintain a great selection of cybersites that can keep any active investor busy. Like games? If so, the Fools will give you plenty of entertainment and challenge. They have games of all sorts to keep you busy and out of trouble. And finally, if you like the bustle of live chatter, the Fools provide chat rooms and scheduled chat events for a variety of live discussions. The Motley Fool forum has become one of the most popular hangouts for investors on AOL. If you're interested in investing with a twist, be sure to drop by the Fools for a good time. It's a great spot for investment information.

ALL ABOUT COMPRESSED FILES

Most files that are available on AOL, other commercial services, and the Internet are compressed, meaning they have been saved in a format that uses significantly less file space. The big advantage is that you can transmit files electronically in a much shorter amount of time than if the files were full size. The format most often used is "zip," which is why many AOL file names are accompanied by the .zip extension, such as graphs.zip and stock.zip.

The big disadvantage of this format is that you have to know how to decompress a file (return it to its full size) before it can be used. Fortunately, the decompression applications are available on AOL too, usually in the form of shareware. Here's a listing of file extensions, the file type, and the utility you need to compress and decompress files.

Extension	File Type	Utility
.arc	binary	arc
.doc	ASCII	none needed
.lzh	binary	lharc
.zip	binary	PKZip
.txt	ASCII	none needed
.gif	binary	none needed
.exe	binary	self-extracting files created by PKZip and lharc
.sit	binary	Stuffit

Can I Really Trade Stocks Online?

 The short answer is a resounding YES! You can find a number of services that will allow you to manage your accounts online, all with varying degrees of flexibility. A number of the commercial brokerage firms provide forums on AOL, including Merrill

Lynch, Fidelity Investments, Vanguard, and T. Rowe Price.

Most, if not all, of these firms will offer online account management. Online transaction processing with AOL offers you a tremendous convenience in that you can manage your investments, access your account information, and make purchases and redemptions of stocks and/or mutual fund shares from one location: right from your PC screen. All of these firms require that you have an established account in order to conduct online transactions, and the process of setting up an initial account typically requires that you fill out application forms and send your initial investments via check through the snail mail, although

Keyword: Fidelity

online applications will become more common in time.

But don't think that you have to have an account with these firms to make use of their online forums. Many provide quality gen-

eral information about investing in stocks and mutual funds in addition to specific information about their own "families of funds," including historical performance data, portfolio information, and fund objectives. Who knows, you may like what you find so much that you'll decide to open an account with all of them.

PCFN and TradePlus

 Although a number of companies offer online stock trading (some through their own proprietary networks, others on the Internet), the two online stock trading services available on AOL at present are the **PC Financial Network** (Keyword "PCFN") and **TradePlus** (Keyword

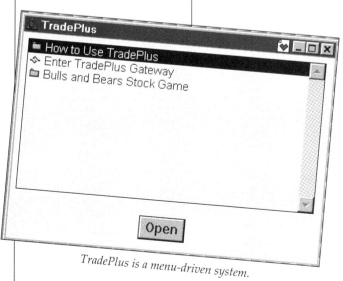

TradePlus is a menu-driven system.

TCP/IP: THE LIFEBLOOD OF THE INTERNET

The mechanism that controls data transfer over the Internet is a network protocol called TCP/IP. A protocol is simply the "language" used by a network to enable communications between computers. In fact, TCP/IP is really two separate protocols that work together to transmit information over a network. TCP stands for "Transmission Control Protocol," and IP stands for "Internet Protocol." A very simplified explanation of the interaction between these protocols is that TCP controls data on the sending and receiving computers, while IP controls the transmission of that data over the network. When you send e-mail over the Internet, for example, the TCP on your computer takes the message and breaks it into smaller pieces, called packets. It then "wraps" each packet in a header, which contains information such as the size of the data, its position in your message, and error control data. Then, the IP routes the packets to the receiving computer over the network.

When a packet arrives at its destination, TCP "unwraps" the packet by reading the header information and checks the error control data to make sure the packet arrived intact. If so, the TCP sends a reply message to the sender indicating that more packets can be sent. If a packet has been corrupted or contains incomplete information, the TCP replies that it should be sent again. When all the packets comprising the message have been received, TCP rebuilds the original message and allows your e-mail program to present the message to you.

PC Financial Network

PC FINANCIAL NETWORK

Save on Commissions

Open an Account Now

Try Our Online Demo

SPECIAL OFFER

Access YOUR ACCOUNT

Keyword: PCFN

"TradePlus"). Both of these companies offer you the ability to buy and sell stocks through interactive menus or screens directly from AOL. And their commissions are deeply discounted from those offered by many full-service brokerages and even other discount brokers. The reason for their lower commission rates? Quite simply, because the level of service offered is minimal compared to that offered by most brokerages.

You will have to ask yourself whether you can manage your own investments without the advice of an investment professional. If you feel that you can take care of your own research and are willing to take your investment portfolio into your own hands, then one of these services may be perfect for you.

PC Financial Network allows you to set up an account online right from AOL. You can also experiment with the service before signing up by trying the PCFN online demo. If you have an account with PCFN, you can check the account's status as well as place buy or sell orders for stocks right through the service. The PCFN interface is a series of graphical, point-and-click screens just like the rest of AOL, so finding your way around, checking your accounts, and placing live trades is easy and straightforward.

PCFN gives you a preview of its commission schedule before you set up an account so you'll know in advance how much your trades will cost. In addition, PCFN has a live demo area where you can practice viewing accounts and trading stocks before you actually sign up for the service. This service is a convenient and cost-effective way to handle your investments without paying large brokerage fees for your transactions.

TradePlus also allows you to manage your investment account directly through its interface on AOL. The TradePlus interface is currently a non-graphical, menu-driven system. This means that instead of pointing and clicking on icons or buttons on the screen, you have to enter menu selections (usually numbers) from your keyboard. While this is somewhat more cumbersome than using a graphical interface, once you get the hang of it you'll find it just as easy and convenient as pointing and clicking your way through the graphical parts of cyberspace.

Currently, you can establish an online account with E*Trade. You'll need to enter the TradePlus gateway to set up or access your account. Once you've established your account, you can place buy or sell orders and check your account's status just as easily as with the PC Financial Network system. The TradePlus system also

offers plenty of online help and instructions to make your investment experience enjoyable.

The service you choose to take advantage of really depends on your investment needs and objectives. Make sure you investigate all your options before signing up with any service. Check into the commission rates, and ask around on some of the message boards for information from other investors. People are usually very happy to share their experiences with various services, and the only cost to you for the information is the effort required to ask.

Learning More

 As you have seen, America Online offers a complete selection of investment services for both the novice and the expert investor. With the arsenal of services available, you should be able to manage all your investments right from your computer and never miss out on any important news or information that could affect your investments. While this book does not provide exhaustive coverage of the services available on AOL and new services are being added continually, by now you have learned enough

about where and how to find information on AOL to make you a much more educated and savvy investor.

If you get lost, you can always start over by going back to the **Personal Finance** screen. Remember, to get to Personal Finance, all you need to type is the keyword "Finance." This screen should be your base of operations for exploring all the various financial and investment-oriented services and forums available on AOL until you discover your favorite places and memorize their keywords, or add them to your **Favorite Places** folder.

A vast amount of information is available for the investor on AOL. Use the information to your advantage, and you're likely to find that the value of your portfolio will increase as your knowledge and experience with investing increases. All the information you need to be a successful investor is just a point and click away.

Of course, America Online is not the only source of financial information in cyberspace. A far more vast territory awaits your exploration in the universe of the Internet. You've already received a basic introduction to the Internet in the first chapter, and perhaps you've already begun to explore by following some of the links on AOL's various financial services that lead you to World Wide Web pages, FTP sites, or Gopher sites.

In the next chapter we'll go into more detail about how to get set up with an Internet service provider (if you choose not to use AOL for your Internet access), and how to find relevant information about investing on the Net. Most of the time the screen shots displayed will show you how various sites look from AOL's current Web browser. But all of these services are available to you from any service provider and through any Web browser. Are you ready to take the plunge? If so, then read on.

SEARCHING FOR INVESTMENT INFORMATION

So far you've learned how to access investment information from America Online. Although AOL is an important part of the Internet, and is a valuable resource with a tremendous selection of services, it's still quite a small section of the Internet. Remember, the Internet is a network of networks, and features information about investing in literally thousands of locations.

Many sites on the Internet are specifically designed to provide investors with useful and important information, but there isn't a central point from which you can explore them, as there was with AOL's Personal Finance Center. To search for Internet resources that are directly related to stocks, mutual funds, and general investing, you can use any Internet connection or any World Wide Web browser.

There are two types of Internet connections: a dedicated connection and a dial-up connection. A dedicated connection is the most direct (and most expensive) of the two; a dial-up connection is indirect and goes through a host (otherwise known as an Internet Service Provider, or ISP for short).

Dedicated Connections

 A dedicated connection provides a direct line to the Internet. There is no waiting for the phone line to be free or for the connection to be open. The Internet is always open and accessible. Dedicated connections to the Internet are the fastest and most expensive, and are used by companies (such as AOL) offering Internet services to clients and customers like you.

How expensive? A small company can expect to pay about $35,000 a year for a direct connection to the Internet, an amount few individuals can afford. Because of the high cost, dedicated connections are usually only available at educational institutions, such as the University of Illinois and Harvard University, as well as at commercial organizations such as Bell Labs, AT&T, and Microsoft. The large institutional connection, in turn, becomes the connection point for thousands of people who work at that ISP.

Dial-Up Connections

 Large organizations often make their dedicated connection available to members via dial-up connections. For instance, if you are a student, faculty member, or researcher, or you work within a university or company that has a connection to the Internet, then you probably can connect, too. From a personal computer at work or at home, you dial up or connect to the host computer, which in turn has a dedicated connection to the Net.

The connections available to individuals who access the Internet through commercial services such as AOL, CompuServe, and Prodigy work this way too. You sign up for an account, and when your account is set up, you dial into your service provider's line, and connect to the Net through their gateway.

To keep up with the tremendous growth of the Internet, information providers (such as AOL) and commercial Internet providers (such as Netcom and Pipeline) now provide connections to the Internet to people with no other way of gaining access.

Commercial Internet Providers

 Using a commercial Internet provider is just like using a

dedicated line, except that the dedicated line belongs to the host (your access provider), who charges you to connect to it. The provider usually supplies the software you need (like the disk that came with this book) as well as technical support, although the quality varies greatly depending upon the provider. In turn, you pay a sign-up fee and/or the monthly and hourly fees. The competition between providers can get intense, and membership deals are always available. You can find out what's being offered by looking through a popular magazine that covers the Net, such as *Wired* magazine.

The quality and capabilities of service providers vary greatly. Some service providers have access to only the most basic of Internet services, such as e-mail. Others provide lots of additional service options, such as a Web browser, Gopher services, FTP, and more. Providers that don't offer a healthy variety will be out of business shortly (unless they upgrade their services) because most consumers want all the Net has to offer.

What's Available

 There are many Internet providers,

and everyone seems to claim the best deal. But as it turns out, market forces are producing some truly great opportunities.

International Discount Telecommunications (IDT) is a good example. There is no charge for online time, and local telephone access is provided in 42 states. There is a flat fee of $19.95 per month, which includes a licensed version of Netscape (the most popular Web browser on the market). When you sign up, International Discount

Telecommunications gives you a local telephone number that's routed to their connection in New Jersey. For more information, contact International Discount Telecommunications, 294 State Street, Hackensack, NJ 07601; or (800) 245-8000.

Following is a list of some other providers you might want to contact. Ask them for written materials and information. Also ask your friends who use the Net how they connect and what providers they recommend:

NETIQUETTE: HOW TO BE NICE ON THE NET

It's up to Internet members like you to adhere to this informally accepted set of guidelines, which make everyone's Internet experience more enjoyable.

- You own your words, so say what you mean and mean what you say. This is especially true with e-mail and newsgroup contributions.

- Foster and respect the ideas of other members. You might disagree with someone's opinion about a book, their view of a raging philosophical debate, or a political opinion, but free exchange of information, without censorship, is one of the primary goals of the Internet.

- Don't intimidate, insult, or verbally abuse anyone. The same good

manners you use in your home and everyday social interactions should be used on the Internet too. Remember, what you post and send by e-mail is often read by more than one recipient.

- Take care not to unintentionally appropriate other people's material. Copyright laws still apply on the Net.

- FLAMING (which includes using all capital letters to express your displeasure) is the online equivalent of yelling or criticizing. Don't do it.

- If you need to download a substantial number of files, try to do it during off-business hours (generally 6:00 p.m. to 8:00 a.m.), when traffic is less congested. But remember, the Internet is a global community, and falls in many different time zones.

- EarthLink Network
  (800) 395-8425

- Netcom
  (800) 353-6600

- Pipeline
  (800) 453-7473

- PSINet
  (800) 419-4932

There are also several major online service providers that offer their

MAKING SENSE OF INVESTMENT LINGO

Not sure what it means when you're "short"? This lingo has nothing to do with your stature; it refers to a specific type of investment, or rather a specific type of position you can hold on a stock. There are several Web sites that will help you understand the difference between a bear market and a bull market, describe the "January effect," and explain most of the other jargon you'll come across.

- *The Wall Street Journal's* Money and Investing Update (http://update. wsj.com) has both a glossary of investment terms and a library of investment information.

- The Laughinstock Investor Dictionary, accessed from the Laughinstock home page, (http:// home.gwp.com/wmartin/index. html) offers a dictionary of terms.

- The Wall Street Words feature on AOL also offers a dictionary of investment terms. Use the keyword "WSW" and click on GO. You'll be able to search for a specific term or browse an alphabetical list.

own services in addition to Internet access. Most of these services provide additional value because their offerings are very well organized and easy to access:

- America Online
  (800) 827-6364

- CompuServe
  (800) 848-8199

- Delphi
  (800) 695-4005

- GEnie
  (800) 638-9636

- The Microsoft Network
  (Available with Windows 95)

- Prodigy
  (800) 776-3449

Here's where you can locate information on different World Wide Web browsers if your Internet connection doesn't provide one:

- Mosaic
  (217) 244-0072

- Netscape
  (415) 254-1900

- Pipeline
  (800) 453-7473

- Spry, Inc.
  (800) 777-9638

If you belong to a professional organization, you already may have a sweet Net deal in the works. For example, Pipeline, a commercial Internet provider in the New York metropol-

itan area, charges $10 per month and includes software that makes the Net user-friendly for members of the Author's Guild. The $10 gives you five hours of free time, and you can buy additional hours for $2 each. Or you can pay $35 a month for unlimited use.

How to Select a Service Provider

 When it comes time to select an Internet service provider, you have many choices about the level and content of service, payment options, and more. As the Internet becomes more and more popular, prices for access will continue to decrease and the services available will continue to increase. At any point, the trick will be to find an ISP that makes you comfortable.

Market forces really drive this industry, so when you're ready to sign up for a particular plan, be sure you've compared one service to another to know you're getting the best deal.

Expect a commercial service to charge a sign-up fee, a monthly fee for access, and probably an hourly fee for the amount of time you're connected to the host computer (beyond a certain minimum, which is usually ten hours). But you can also expect these services to offer specials, such as a waived sign-up fee, reduced online costs, and other incentives to join or stay with that service. For example, Netcom gives you unlimited Internet hours for a flat fee of $19.95 per month, and they may even waive the $25 sign-up fee.

If the service provider doesn't have a local phone number where you make the initial contact to sign onto their computer, you'll also be charged for the cost of the call itself. Even when the commercial Internet provider uses a special long-distance company such as SprintNet, phone time can cost $8 or more per hour.

Make sure you get the services you want for the price you want to pay and that your connection is reliable and regularly available. There's no benefit if your provider saves you five bucks a month on fees, but its servers are always down! Also try calling the ISP customer service number to make sure that the reps are willing and able to help you solve problems.

Questions to Ask When Selecting a Service Provider

 Want to know what you could (or should) ask an Internet provider before you sign up? Consider these questions:

How much will this cost?
- What is the hourly connect charge, if any?
- If there is a sign-up or start-up fee, is it a one-time fee or an annual fee?
- What is the monthly fee?
- Are there any extra service charges?
- Is there a discounted hourly charge for connections made during off-business hours?
- Is there a discount for volume use?
- Are there different costs for different-speed modems?
- Are there discounts for members of particular organizations?

What does the service offer?
- What basic services (such as e-mail, FTP, Web browser, and so on) are provided?
- Does the provider offer access to other commercial services (so you can

PAPER ISN'T DEAD YET

Although the Internet and online services like AOL offer tremendous value to the investor, you can still benefit from traditional investment publications and newsletters. Many daily and weekly publications provide in-depth articles and information that may not yet be available online or are not always accessible. For example, it's still difficult to download the latest news on the commuter train every morning!

Keep in mind that although some of the publications are available at your newsstand or library, many specialized newsletters are available only by subscription. And some of the subscription fees can be rather expensive. But consider these when you're not plugged in:

Business Week

Forbes Magazine

Fortune Magazine

Individual Investor

Investor's Business Daily

Kiplinger's Personal Finance Magazine

Money Magazine

Moody's Handbook of Common Stocks

Personal Investment Magazine

Standard & Poor's Stock Reports

The Value Line Investment Survey

The Wall Street Journal

Zacks Analyst Watch

send e-mail to your friends and colleagues, even if you're not on the same service)?

- Are there different types of accounts available, at different rates for different categories of users, such as individuals, companies, and so on?

- Can you open an account just to use e-mail?

- What modem speeds are available?

- What software is available for connecting to the Internet?

- How many customers does the provider have?

- Is there a local phone line in your area with which you can connect? If not, how will you connect from a remote site, and how much will it cost?

- Does the service offer storage space for down-

loaded files? How much space? What does it cost to keep documents in storage?

- Are practice or tutorial exercises available? Does it cost anything to use these?

What about technical support?

- Is online technical support available? Can you ask questions on forums

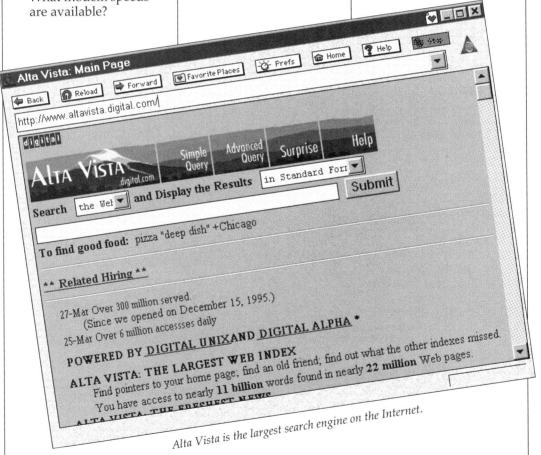

Alta Vista is the largest search engine on the Internet.

or any major bulletin boards?

- Is phone support available?

- Is there a charge for technical phone support? Is there a toll-free number?

Finding Useful Information

 By now, you should have an idea of how vast the Internet is. When you're looking for information to help you make wise investment decisions, there really isn't a single place on the Net that is the best investor's choice. The good

news is that you can find tons of information on most Internet sites that are dedicated to providing investment information. And you can always use one of the search engines listed in chapter one to find information on investments.

As you get to one of the sites used to search the Internet, you may wonder exactly how to use it! Once you become familiar with the searching process, you'll find that it becomes quite easy to discover exactly what you're looking for, if it's out there. Try exploring one of the search

sites now. Go into your Web browser and enter the URL for **Alta Vista** in the text area at the top of the screen. Following are the most widely used search sites, with their URLs in parentheses. If you're using AOL for Internet access, you can use the Keyword command

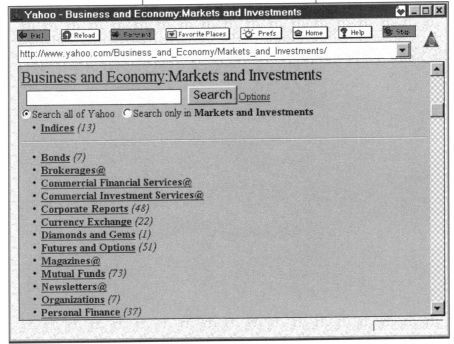

Yahoo! can point the way to a tremendous amount of investment information.

(**CTRL-K**) to get to the Keyword screen, then you can enter the URL directly and click on **GO** to get to the search site. Once again, here are the addresses of the search engines:

- **Alta Vista**
  (http://www.altavista.digital.com)
- **Yahoo!**
  (http://www.yahoo.com)
- **Excite**
  (http://www.excite.com)
- **Lycos**
  (http://www.lycos.com)
- **OpenText**
  (http://www.opentext.com)
- **Infoseek NetSearch**
  (http://www.infoseek.com)
- **WebCrawler**
  (http://www.webcrawler.com)

Each search engine works differently, has its own strengths and weaknesses, and is continually being updated with new sites. So the search engine you choose will ultimately depend on your preferences. Typically, you can do a simple search by entering a word or phrase into the text box on the search engine's screen and clicking on the **Submit** or **Send** button. For example, if you enter

"Investments" into Alta Vista's search screen and click on **Submit,** you'll find about 100,000 matching links! The word "Invest" returns over 100,000 hits, and the word "Investing" returns about 70,000.

Narrowing the Search

 As you spend more time on the Internet, you'll soon discover that there will never be enough time to find everything that might possibly interest you. For example, the Alta Vista search engine (which at this writing is the largest single index of information) contains data on over 11 million Internet sites! While browsing through all the potential documents retrieved by a search engine may prove to be interesting and rewarding in the long run, there will be times when you'll want to find something specific quickly, without reading through everything.

The way to do this with a search engine is to learn to ask the right questions. Most of the search engines on the Internet allow you to search for more specific information by structuring your request, or query, in such a way that you can narrow down the list of possible matches. Alta Vista allows you to search

by using either a simple query or an advanced query by following a few rules. Each search engine has a link to its own help system, where you can learn the specific rules that apply to that location. However, most query engines use very similar rules, and you should be able to narrow your searches on any search engine by composing your queries carefully.

For assistance with the search syntax on Alta Vista, click on the section labeled **Help** on the picture bar at the top of the screen. Some of the common rules that your search engine may use include:

- Start by typing a single word in the search box. The search engine will try to find all documents in its database that contain this word.

- Use lowercase letters unless you are looking for something that has to have a specific case in its lettering. Using a combination of capital and lowercase letters often limits the search unnecessarily.

- Use double-quotes to search for words in a phrase. So, to find information about investment banking firms, type "investment banking firms" and then click on the **Submit** button. If you don't sur-round the phrase in quotes, the search will return documents that contain any of the three words, "investment," "banking," or "firms," and you'll wind up with a huge list of irrelevant documents.

- Use the plus sign (+) before a word or phrase to make sure it is used in every one of the returned documents. For example, if you want to find information on discount brokerage firms, you could enter:

  "brokerage firms" + dis-count

- Use a minus sign (–) to make sure a specific word or phrase does not end up in the list of hits. If you wanted to find brokerage firms that were not discount bro-kers, you could enter:

  "brokerage firms" – dis-count

- Search for a number of items by separating the search words with a comma, semicolon, colon, or other punctua-tion. For example, you could search for "investments, stocks, mutual funds" and the search results would include documents hav-ing any or all of these words or phrases.

- Search for information using characters that are considered "wild card" characters. These are characters that can have any meaning, just like a wild card in a card game can represent any card in the deck.

  Wild cards are usually characters like the aster-isk (*), the percent sign (%), or the question mark (?). The search command "invest*" will return documents with the word "investor," "investments," "invest-ing," "invested," and so on. If you aren't careful, you'll wind up with a really huge list of results!

- Search for multiple words that occur any-where in the document by entering your query like this:

  "broker AND customer"

  The word AND in this query is called an oper-ator, because it operates on the two words in the query. Other operators often used are:

- OR to return documents containing at least one of the words.

- NOT to exclude words or phrases from the query.

- NEAR to find words in close proximity to each other. In Alta Vista this will return documents in which the two search words are within at least ten words of each other.

- Prioritize the results. Some search engines allow you to use paren-theses to group words or phrases together. Others, like Alta Vista, allow you to rank the priority of documents.

You'll need to keep in mind that these are just general rules and that each search service will have slightly different methods for finding information. Make sure you click on the link to **Help** so you can get full information on the specific rules used by the particular search engine you are visiting.

Internet Search Engines

 The seven search engines listed here are the primary search tools in use on the Internet today. Of course, as the Internet grows and expands, additional search services will probably become available. As you are already aware, each search engine is unique and has its own strengths and weaknesses. Here's an overview of what they offer:

Alta Vista . This is (http://www. altavista.digital.com) is

WHAT'S A HOME PAGE?

As you become more familiar with the Internet, you'll frequently hear the term *home page*. A home page is the opening screen of a Web site, and you get there by entering the appropriate URL in your Web browser. Some home pages are very fancy and attractive, but creating a standard home page is actually as easy as typing a letter. All you need to learn are the basics of *hypertext markup language* (HTML).

An HTML file is created using descriptive tags to identify how the text, graphic images, and sound will be displayed on a screen. These tags are used in pairs, and are embedded in a document before and after the content. For example, <h1> is the tag to identify the start of the highest level subhead (<\h1> identifies the end), and <p> is the tag to begin a new paragraph—something like this:

<h1>My First Home Page<\h1><p>

When a browser such as Netscape, Mosaic, or NetCruiser reads the file for this home page, it converts it into the graphic and text images you see on the screen. You can learn more about HTML at:

http://www.ncsa.uiuc.edu/General/Internet/WWW/HTMLPrimer.html

One of the best programs available to create HTML documents is Assistant Pro 2, from Brooklyn North Software. For more information contact: harawitz@fox.nstn.ns.ca or 25 Doyle Street, Bedford, Nova Scotia, Canada B4A IK4.

currently the largest database of Web sites that is indexed for searching and available to the public. All that information can be overwhelming to sort through, so try to be very specific when you define your search parameters. One very nice feature of Alta Vista is the **Advanced Search** area, where you can enter more complex queries using operators such as AND, OR, and NOT. If you structure your query well, Alta Vista will find a very good selection of documents for you to explore.

You can specify what area of the Internet you want to search (for instance, the Web or Usenet newsgroups) by using the drop-down feature. To do this, click on the arrow next to a menu item, and you will see a drop-down list of options.

Alta Vista also has a random link generator, which means you can click on the **Surprise** button at the top of the page, and you will be given a short list of unrelated topics. Click on one, and you can explore a randomly selected site!

Yahoo! The most attractive feature of Yahoo! (http://www.yahoo.com) is its extensive directory of links to other sites.

Although some other search sites provide topical lists of links to interesting places, the list for investors on Yahoo! probably has the most extensive collection of links to investment-related information available today. If you really want to get serious about exploring investment-related sites on the Net, visit Yahoo!, and click on the **Investments** link located under the **Business and Economy** topic. The subjects available cover a wide variety of investment topics:

- Bonds
- Commercial Financial Services
- Corporate Reports
- Currency Exchange
- Diamonds and Gems
- Personal Finance
- Precious Metals
- Real Estate
- Stocks

Another very interesting (and useful!) feature of Yahoo! is that it will allow you to search another search engine by clicking on a link at the bottom of the screen. So for example, if you do a search on Yahoo! for a particular topic and aren't satisfied with the results, you can click on the **Alta Vista** link at the bottom of the screen. Yahoo! will not only

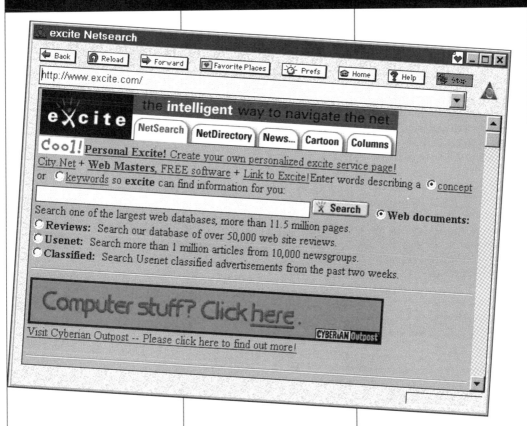

launch Alta Vista for you, but it will also pass your query on to the other engine and run the query. This is a great feature because it allows you to build a single query and use it on multiple search engines.

Excite. Excite (http://www.excite.com) offers search functions that are similar to those found in Alta Vista, but it also allows you to limit your searches to certain categories.

When you arrive at the Excite home page, you'll notice a series of tabs at the top of the screen. The default tab is **NetSearch.** Use it to start a general search, or target your search to specific areas by clicking on the following option buttons:

- Web Documents
- Reviews
- Usenet
- Classified

If you want to limit your search, click on the **Concept** or **Keyword** buttons. A concept-based search attempts to interpret the meaning of your query and returns appropriate documents.

The **Net Directory** tab at the top of the screen takes you to a page that has a listing of categories. Among the categories listed there, you will discover one called **Business** and another called **Money and Investing.** If you click on either of these links, you'll move to more specific listings of categories, such as **Investing** or **Real Estate.** When you continue to

SECURITY ISSUES ON THE INTERNET

A great concern to many Internet users is the security of information transmitted online. Everyone has heard about hackers who get hold of sensitive government or corporate databases, or who steal credit card numbers and other personal material. Although it is true that you should be careful with the information you transmit on the Internet, some of the worries may be exaggerated. Use common sense. For example, don't ever give your passwords to people you don't know, even if they claim to be employees of your service provider. If you have difficulty accessing your account, contact your service provider directly to set up a new password or account.

Many sites that allow you to purchase merchandise or place investment transactions over the Internet require you to use a security-enhanced browser like Netscape or Microsoft Internet Explorer. While it is possible for someone to get your credit card number if you transmit it over a nonsecure Web browser, consider that you hand it over to clerks, gas station attendants, and waitstaff on a daily basis. Any of them could misuse your number, and far more easily. In general, most people are honest and won't abuse your trust. It is probably safe to purchase products from known vendors online, but don't ever give out your password or credit card numbers to people who contact you by e-mail or in a chat area.

The Lycos home page

select more specific categories, you can eventually narrow your search to a large number of interesting sites that directly relate to your subject.

The option tabs at the top of the screen include:

- News
- Cartoons
- Columns

Lycos. This engine (http://www.lycos.com) offers the same type of word or phrase searches as the others. But its home page has a series of links that allow you to move directly to links that cover your subject, without requiring specific search parameters. Lycos calls this feature **A2Z** because its coverage is so broad. For topics of interest to

investors, you can click on the **Business & Investing** link to go to another page that lists many investment-related topics.

Lycos also reviews Web sites in its Point service. Simply click on **Point** on the Lycos logo at the top of the screen. Another interesting feature is its **New 2 Net** service that provides information about new Internet sites in cyberspace. It's a great place to explore interesting links!

OpenText. The Open Text engine (http://www.opentext.com) has a home page that allows you to search its site using a search text box.

If you want to search the entire Internet for information, click on the little tri-

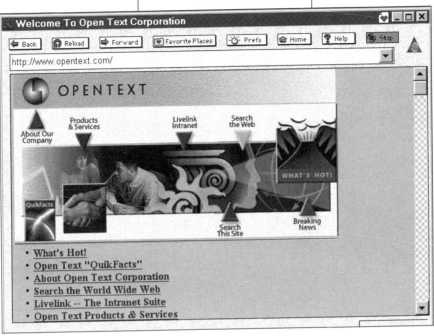

A sample OpenText search screen.

angle at the top of the screen that is labeled **Search the Web.** The **OpenText** Web search engine makes it very easy to construct a query that will find the information you are seeking.

As you can see from the sample OpenText screen, the process of creating a query, even a complex one, is dramatically simplified by the use of text boxes (where you can enter information) and drop-down list boxes (where you simply select information). Although OpenText is not quite as complex or feature-filled as some of the other search engines, the query-building feature is a

tremendous asset when you are first learning how to create search queries.

Infoseek NetSearch. This engine (http://www.infoseek.com) offers both basic search functions and a list of topics to browse through on its home page. In addition, the home page includes helpful hints and search tips so you don't have to click around to other areas of the site to get assistance with creating queries. It also offers a drop-down list.

WebCrawler. The WebCrawler (http://www.webcrawler.com) is the search engine that is AOL's default search

tool on its Web browser. (You were briefly introduced to WebCrawler in chapter one.) Currently, it offers the most basic service of all the search engines listed here. You can search by word or phrase in the text box, and select the number of matches that the search engine should return. You can also specify whether the search should return documents containing all the words you entered or any of the words you entered.

This search engine is great for quick scans on a keyword or two because it is not very complex, and it returns results quickly. It is also very convenient to get

Explore
these popular
Infoseek Select
topics:

Search for information about:

 in the World Wide Web Search Now

Infoseek Guide is best viewed with:

Arts &
Entertainment ◄

Business &
Finance ◄

Computers &
Internet ◄

Education ◄

Government &
Politics ◄

Health &

Basic Search Tips:

- Click in the box above and type a few words that describe what you want to find. For example, typing **growing orchids indoors** will find sites about caring for orchids.

- If you are looking for a person or place, type the name, starting with capital letters. For example, typing **Florence Italy** will find sites

---

to when you are in AOL, because you don't have to remember or type in a URL. Just go to the Internet Center, and click your way over to the WebCrawler!

This general description of each of the major search sites available on the Internet should help you get started in your search for investment information. If you simply want to explore a number of different locations to see what each contains, you should probably start with sites that contain predefined lists of topics, such as InfoSeek, Lycos, or Yahoo!

These allow you to browse many other sites that are valuable to investors. For instance, click on links to **Business, Investing,** or anything similar.

Finding Investment-Related Newsgroups

 You've seen in chapter one how to use AOL's **Search All Newsgroups** feature to find Usenet newsgroups that may be of interest to you. As a refresher, here are the steps to get to this feature:

- Press **CTRL-K,** or select **Go To** from the AOL

menu, then select **Keyword.**

- Enter "Newsgroups" in the text area of the Keyword screen.

- Click on the **GO** button.

From the Newsgroups screen, you can click on the **Search All Newsgroups** button to search all the available newsgroups that AOL offers. To find newsgroups relating to investments:

- In the search text box, enter a word such as "finance," "investments," or "invest."

- Click on the **Search** button.

Surprisingly, there really aren't that many newsgroups on the Internet relating to investment topics, but the ones that are available tend to have quite a bit of activity. Probably the busiest newsgroup relating to investment topics is misc.invest.stocks, a newsgroup that gets hundreds of new postings every day. This newsgroup is a hub of activity for all sorts of investors, from the most seasoned professional to the newest of the newbies!

The diversity of individuals participating in discussions on Internet newsgroups makes for very interesting chatter, and you can always learn something from the messages posted. You'll also learn about other useful Internet sites from the Usenet discussions, because people are always posting information about new Web sites, mailing lists, and discussion groups. As always, do your homework before you follow any leads, and remember to use your judgment about any information you receive. Usenet newsgroups, just like the message boards on AOL, are a mix of good, solid information, scams, hypesters, and snake oil salespersons.

A list of investment-related newsgroups.

If you already know the name of a newsgroup you want to visit frequently, add it to your list by following these directions:

- Go to your Keyword screen (**CTRL-K**).

- Type "Newsgroups" then click on **Go.**

- Click on the **Expert Add** button.

- Enter the Internet address of the newsgroup. For example,

  misc.invest.stocks.

- Click on the **Add** button to add the newsgroup to your list.

The **Expert Add** screen also has a button called **Latest Newsgroups,** which lists newsgroups that have recently been created on the Internet. You can browse this list to see if there's anything of interest to you, then click on **List Subjects** to view a list of topics in the selected news-

group, **Read Messages** to read all current messages, **Add** to add the selected item to your list of newsgroups, or **More** to list more newsgroups, if they don't all fit on one screen.

If you want to search another site for information on Usenet newsgroups, try the **Tile.Net** Web site. This site maintains an enormous list of all newsgroups that are available on the Net. You can either search the site, or you can click on topics that will take you to listings of newsgroups that fit particular categories. To get to Tile.Net's index of investment-related sites:

On AOL, press **CTRL-K** to get to your Keyword screen. If you aren't on AOL, open your browser and establish your connection to your service provider:

- Enter this URL in the

Keyword screen, or in the text box at the top of your browser:

http://www.tile.net/tile/news/index.html

- Click on **Index**

- Scroll down the list to the letter **I** and click on that link.

- Scroll down the list of topics until you arrive at **Invest**, then click on that link.

Finding Investment-Related Mailing Lists

 In chapter one you were introduced to the eINVEST listserve mailing list. Although at the present time there aren't many investment-related mailing lists, you can find some good lists by using the Internet Information service called **Inter-Links.** To get to this Web site from AOL:

- Press **CTRL-K** to get to your Keyword screen. (If you aren't on AOL, open your browser and establish your connection to your service provider.)

- Enter the following URL:

http://www.nova.edu/Inter-Links/

- Click on the **Basic Internet Services** link.

- In the **On-line Discussions** section, click on the **Electronic Mailing Lists** link.

The **E-Mail Discussion Groups** page contains a number of very helpful links that allow you to search for mailing lists that match your criteria, or view lists of mailing lists that you can join. There are also links to help files and information about using mailings lists and listserve. If you click on **Search List of Discussion Groups (Inter-Links)**, you'll be able to enter a Keyword to search on. If you enter the word "Invest", you'll retrieve a list of mailing lists that include:

- Small Investors

- Environmental Investment Priorities in Asia

- Trading Cards

- eINVEST

- Student Managed Investment Funds

- Oil and Gas Investments

- Real Estate Broker

You will also notice that the Keyword search also returns a number of mailing lists that are not necessarily relevant to investors, such as "A Forum for Poets." That's because the description for the mailing list includes the word "investigating." You can limit this type of extraneous listing by making the Keyword search more specific.

The Inter-Links home page also can direct you to resources other than mailing lists, such as Usenet newsgroups, Web sites, and other useful indexes using the Inter-Links.

WEB SITES & NEWSGROUPS FOR INVESTORS

ALTHOUGH THE INTERNET OFFERS SOME POWERFUL tools for finding investment-related sites, it's helpful to keep track of resources that you know you can count on. This chapter begins by explaining how to access your favorite sites quickly every time you get online. Later you'll read about some of the best investment resources online.

Keeping Track of Favorite Places from AOL

 You can always make your way to the sites you want through AOL's Personal Finance Center, but as you find places that you think you'll want to visit again, you can add them to your list of favorite places. Here's how:

- Highlight the URL at the top of the screen.

- Click on the **heart** icon at the top right of the Web browser screen.

- Click on **Yes** when AOL asks if you want to add this to your list.

It's as simple as that! Any time you want to go back to that site, just click on the **Favorite Places** heart, and then double-click on the name of the site you want

to visit. This way, you'll build up a library of your most useful Internet and AOL sites over time.

Keeping Track of Favorite Sites on the Internet

 On the Internet, your only real "home" is your Web browser, and you have to get used to entering URLs or clicking through several layers of Web links. Fortunately, you can learn to store and organize the URLs to your favorite Web sites because most browsers offer **Bookmarks** or other methods to keep track of those links.

If you aren't comfortable or satisfied with the Favorite Places feature of AOL (or the comparable feature of other browsers), and you have a more advanced browser such as **Netscape Navigator** or **Microsoft Internet Explorer,** you can find Web sites that allow you to create your own customized home page. (The browser in version 2.5 of AOL doesn't support customizable home pages, but future versions of the AOL software will.)

Then you can set your browser to load that default home page first every time you go to the Internet. You can put links to your favorite investment sites

on your custom home page and use it as your home base for exploring the Internet.

To create a custom home page, try this:

- **Customize This Page,** offered by The Microsoft Network at http://www.msn.com

- **The Personal Excite Service,** offered by Excite at http://www.excite.com

- **Personal Workspace,** offered by Netscape at http://www.netscape.com

To create your custom page at each site, follow the link that leads you to the home page customization option:

- On the Microsoft Network home page, click on the **Customize This Page** link.

- On Excite, follow the link to **Personal Excite.**

- On Netscape, click on the **My Page** link.

Each site is a little different, but usually all you have to do is fill out a form online. You can enter links to Web or Usenet addresses by filling in a few text boxes on the form, and you can select various news and information sources to appear on your page by

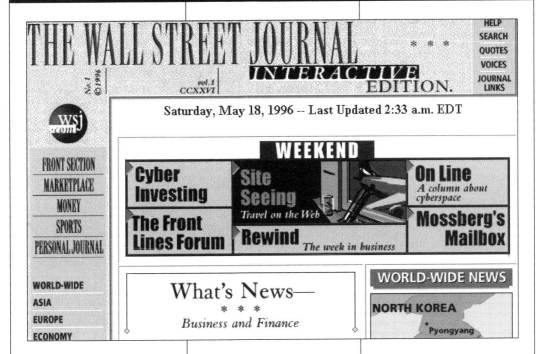

THE WALL STREET JOURNAL INTERACTIVE EDITION.

No.1 ©1996 · vol.1 CCXXVI

HELP
SEARCH
QUOTES
VOICES
JOURNAL
LINKS

Saturday, May 18, 1996 -- Last Updated 2:33 a.m. EDT

FRONT SECTION
MARKETPLACE
MONEY
SPORTS
PERSONAL JOURNAL

WORLD-WIDE
ASIA
EUROPE
ECONOMY

WEEKEND

Cyber Investing

Site Seeing
Travel on the Web

On Line
A column about cyberspace

The Front Lines Forum

Rewind *The week in business*

Mossberg's Mailbox

What's News—
* * *
Business and Finance

WORLD-WIDE NEWS

NORTH KOREA
★ Pyongyang

clicking on check boxes for a series of options. The customizable home pages also allow you to select the background color or pattern of your custom home page and select your choice of stock quotes to appear.

When you are finished setting up your custom home page, use your browser's preferences or options menu to make the URL of your custom page the default.

Some of the Best Investment Sites on the Net

 All investment sites are not created

equal. Some sites are wonderful, information-packed cyberplaces where you can spend hours and never run out of exciting discoveries. Other sites turn out to be little more than advertisements for products or services. Here's an introduction to some of the best resources for investment information on the Web. Many of the services are free, but sometimes you will be required to register and pay a subscription fee. You'll have to decide whether the fees offer a good value for your needs.

The Wall Street Journal

 One good site to explore is The Wall Street Journal's

Interactive Edition, the online version of the venerable news source. Although the site is available only by subscription for $49, there may be opportunities for free trial periods. To get to The Wall Street Journal's Interactive Edition on the web, search for this URL:

http://interactive.wsj. com/

You'll get to the Journal's introductory screen, where you can register by clicking on the **Subscribe** link. This will take you to another page, where you can select the type of Web browser you'll be using to access the Interactive Edition. If you are using a security-enabled browser like Microsoft Internet Explorer or Netscape Navigator, you should click on the **Secure** link; otherwise click on the **Open** link. These links will lead you to an application and a few questions that will help *The Wall Street Journal* maintain some demographic information about subscribers. These questions are fairly standard and include such things as:

- How many stock transactions have you made in the past 12 months?

- What is your profession?

A MICROHISTORY OF THE NEW YORK STOCK EXCHANGE

People have gathered in a central place to exchange goods and services for thousands of years. But the idea of exchanging shares of ownership in an organization or company is only a few hundred years old. An early version of the New York Stock Exchange (NYSE) was organized in 1792 when a group of 24 brokers met under a buttonwood tree on Wall Street (so the legend goes) to establish a trade securities agreement and to charge a uniform commission rate to their customers. The agreement signed by these gentlemen is known as the *Buttonwood Agreement.* The NYSE wasn't officially established until 1817, when brokers created the New York Stock & Exchange Board (NYS&EB). Read about the New York Stock Exchange's history at http://www.nyse.com.

- What Web browser are you using to access *The Wall Street Journal*?

- What type of Internet connection do you have?

When you've completed the form, click on the **Submit** button at the bottom of the screen. After you've read a long legal statement and disclaimer, click on the **I accept** button, and you're ready to go.

Once your registration has been accepted, you can explore *The Wall Street Journal*'s online service any time by entering your user name and password in the logon screen.

The Wall Street Journal's Interactive Edition offers the same comprehensive news coverage that you have come to expect from the print edition including the following:

Interactive Edition's Front Page. This page contains the headlines for the day, in a format that is similar to the front page of the printed version of *The Wall Street Journal.* On the left-hand side of the page, you'll be able to read a short synopsis of the day's headlines in the **What's News** column. The right-hand column contains important news stories and

updates, such as the current state of the various markets, international and national news and events, coverage of political events, and so on. Most of the headlines are accompanied by links that take you right to the full text of those stories. It is much more convenient to read than printed newspapers, which break the stories across several pages!

The Interactive Edition's Front Page also includes image maps at the top, bottom, and left sides of the screen. You can use any of these image maps to navigate your way through the entire text of the Journal online. Some of the links at the top of the page include:

Help. Need some assistance finding your way around the Journal? Click on this link on the image map and you'll find everything you need to make your experience a positive one. You can get an online tour of the site and read the FAQs for the Interactive Edition, or you can get help on navigating the site in general.

Search. Allows you to search the Journal for articles and stories of interest to you. You'll also find a couple of the terrific features specifically geared to investors. For example, when you click on **Search,**

the page that appears provides links to:

- **Briefing Books.** This service is an invaluable resource for information about individual companies that you may want to invest in. A Briefing Book is created for you by the Journal when you enter a company name or ticker symbol and click on the **Get Briefing Book** button.

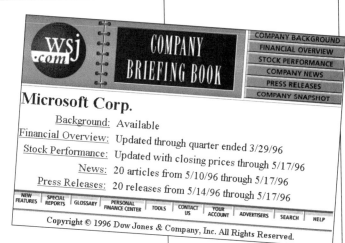

A Briefing Book contains background information about the company's business objectives, a financial overview of the company, a chart of the company's stock performance, and links to any news or press releases about the company that have been printed in the Dow Jones news service. You'll also notice that at the bottom of the Briefing Book screen, there are links to other features of the Interactive Edition.

- **Index to Market Data.** If you click on this link on the **Search** page, you'll get to a page that is filled with links to market data of all sorts, listed in the following categories:

U.S. Stock Markets
Find information about the most actively traded stocks for the day, or

the biggest percentage gainers or losers in the market. You'll also be able to get dividend information on stocks, plus listings of new stocks and securities listings.

World Stock Markets
Indexes for world stock markets, as well as information on leading or lagging international stock groups (for example, Asian stocks or European stocks). You'll also find information listed alphabetically by country.

Commodities Markets
Information on commodities futures, as well as statistics and prices for various commodities, such as grains or oilseeds, livestock and meats, metals and petroleum, and so on.

Credit Markets
Money rates, treasury

quotes, Federal Reserve data, and other credit and money-market information are available by clicking on the links in this section.

Foreign Exchange
Continuous updates on the exchange rates of various currencies.

Mutual Funds
The **Mutual Fund Scorecards** link lists hundreds of funds in every conceivable category and provides historical performance data, net asset values, costs involved with investing, and other useful information for mutual fund investors. The **Closed-End Funds** link offers information on closed-end funds of every type.

Quotes. Get quick stock or mutual fund quotes either by ticker symbol or by

THE WALL STREET JOURNAL INTERACTIVE EDITION — MONEY & INVESTING

Sunday, May 19, 1996

HELP
SEARCH
QUOTES
VOICES

wsj.com

FRONT SECTION
MARKETPLACE
MONEY
SPORTS
PERSONAL JOURNAL

DATA BANK
U.S. STOCKS
SMALL U.S. STOCKS
STOCKS IN THE AMERICAS
STOCKS IN ASIA
STOCKS IN EUROPE
HEARD ON THE STREET
CREDIT MARKETS
FOREIGN EXCHANGE
COMMODITIES

Industrials Finish Just Shy of Record, As Bonds Rally

By DAVE PETTIT
INTERACTIVE EDITION

The Dow Jones Industrial Average climbed to just short of a record on Friday, tracking a rally in the bond market. The dollar barely moved

Dow Jones Industrial Average
at five-minute intervals

5700
5690
5680
5670
5660
5650
5640
5630

Friday, at close
5687.50, up 52.45

3:30 10:30 11:30 12:30 1:30 2:30 3:30
Prior day's close

Will Investors Buy New Indexed Bonds?

The U.S. Treasury plans

- Law
- Who's News

Money. The Money section is the primary resource for investors on the Journal's Interactive Edition. Here you'll find articles, stories, and editorials relating to all aspects of money and investing, including:

- **Data Bank.** A one-stop resource for gathering statistical information on the markets and the indexes used to track the performance of those markets, clearly arranged in table format and categorized. At the bottom of this page you'll also find links to the **Index to Market Data** mentioned above, as well as **Most Active Stocks, Percentage Gainers, Percentage Losers,** and **Dow Jones Averages Charts.**

- **U.S. Stocks.** Articles and links to information about domestic stocks and companies.

- **Small U.S. Stocks.** Basically the same type of information that is provided on the U.S. Stocks page, except that the focus is on small-capitalization stocks.

- **Stocks in the Americas.** News and information regarding stocks and company activity in Canada, Mexico, and Central and South

name. When you get quotes, you'll also get a brief company snapshot and a link to that company's Briefing Book. This page also allows you to set up and track your own portfolio of up to 30 investments.

Voices. This is the most "interactive" part of the Interactive Edition! Here you can send messages to the Journal's editors and participate in chats and discussion groups on many topics.

Journal Links. Links to information referred to in the print editions of *The Wall Street Journal.*

The left-hand image map has many links to general news items. The links that

will help investors most are:

Marketplace. The Marketplace section is the part of the Journal that primarily focuses on information relating to business news and the various investment markets. On the left-hand side of the Marketplace page, you'll find a number of links that are oriented to business and investing. Each of these links leads to a news and information page that deals with the specific topics indicated. The links available here include:

- Technology
- Marketing and Media
- Health & Science
- Business Focus

America. You'll also find information here on market indexes for various American markets.

- **Stocks in Asia.** Information about the markets in Asia, various Asian companies, and index information.

- **Stocks in Europe.** Information about the markets in Europe, various European companies, and index information.

- **Heard on the Street.** This is the Journal's hot news and opinions section. Interesting editorials and articles offer insight and perspective for investors. This area also includes links to previous Heard on the Street articles in the Journal's archives.

- **Credit Markets.** Articles and information about the various credit markets.

- **Foreign Exchange.** Foreign exchange rates and information.

- **Commodities.** Futures and prices on the commodities markets, stories and articles, and links to more information.

- **Mutual Funds.** Overviews and articles relating to the mutual fund industry, plus links to the **Mutual Fund Scorecards, Closed-End Funds,** and the mutual fund **Quarterly Review.**

- **Personal Finance.** Information specifically designed to assist the individual investor, including articles and stories of interest, plus links to the Personal Finance Center and the BanxQuote Banking Center, an online banking information service.

Economy. The Economy page is where you'll find important economic data that can affect your investments. This page offers news and articles relating to the current state of the U.S. economy, including budget information, the trade deficit, gross domestic product, unemployment information, and much more.

At the bottom of each screen is another image map (see below) that has links to additional information services offered by *The Wall Street Journal:*

New Features. Lists new services and features offered by the Journal's online service.

Special Reports. This is a column unto itself on the resources page and heads a list of links to interesting **Wall Street Journal Special Reports.** These reports include polls, summaries of market information, year-end analyses, reports on technology and entertainment, and many other reports as they become available.

Glossary. The alphabet as a series of hot-links! Click on a letter to find definitions of all sorts of terms relating to the news and investments.

Personal Finance Center. A comprehensive library of information on numerous different investment-related topics. This area is a complete personal finance resource that covers such topics as:

- College
- College Financing
- Employee Benefits
- Estate Planning
- Financial Planning

| NEW FEATURES | SPECIAL REPORTS | GLOSSARY | PERSONAL FINANCE CENTER | TOOLS | CONTACT US | YOUR ACCOUNT | ADVERTISERS |

- Home and Auto
- Investing
- Mutual Funds
- Retirement Planning
- Stocks
- Taxes

Tools. Need a plug-in for your browser to be able to view (or hear!) a particular type of information? Click on the **Tools** link to find many of these resources available for you to download immediately.

Contact Us. Contact the editors of *The Wall Street Journal* with your questions, suggestions, or comments.

Your Account. Change your personal account information, such as your password, user name, address information, and so on.

Advertisers. Links to the companies that have placed ads on the Interactive Edition of the Journal.

The quality and quantity of information available from the Journal is unparalleled, and the site is rich with links to all sorts of resources. The site is also very well organized and easy to navigate, making your search for investment information very reward-

ing. And you'll find all the other sections that are offered by the print version of the Journal, such as Politics & Policy, Leisure & Arts, and the Weather.

NETworth

 Are you more interested in mutual funds than individual stocks? If so, you'll want to check out the **NETworth** Web site. This site offers information on over 5,000 mutual funds, from net asset values to portfolio information, and it offers links to other sites that cover mutual funds, stocks, and equities. To get to NETworth, enter: http://networth.galt.com/

There is no charge for access to the information. However, some areas of NETworth's Web site are accessible only to individuals who have registered. When you get to the Networth home page, click the **Free Registration** button on the image map at the top of the page. This will allow you to fill out an online form with some basic information about yourself. When you've completed the form, click on the **Submit** button, and you'll be registered with a temporary User ID. NETworth will send you an e-mail message when your User ID is registered.

NETworth has a very well-balanced collection of information for all kinds of investors and offers several customization options as well, so you can make the data display fit your requirements. The services from NETworth are all available from the home page either by clicking on links or by clicking on icons at the top of the screen. Once you've selected a topic, you'll find numerous additional subtopics. Some of the services offered by NETworth include the following:

The Mutual Fund Market Manager. This area is billed by NETworth as "today's finest, most sophisticated offering of online funds information," and it may not be an overstatement! This area offers a number of mutual fund services, all of which are available by clicking links on the home page or on the image map at the top of the page.

Fund Search. This feature is directly available on the **Mutual Fund Market Manager** page. Simply enter a fund's symbol or name in the text boxes that appear on the screen, then click on the **Get NAV/Profile** button. You'll get the current market price per share of the fund, as well as an informational synopsis of the

View the winners' list

NETworth Main Menu

FREE Registration
What's New at NETworth?

fund itself. A great, quick information feature!

Fund Atlas. A comprehensive overview of thousands of mutual funds. This is the place where you can find information and historical data for mutual funds of all kinds. The main page offers a "top 25" list of the best-performing mutual funds, based on a time period and fund type that you can specify by using drop-down list boxes. Links to fund groups, individual funds, and a comprehensive fund search feature are all available from the Fund Atlas.

Meet the Experts. This page offers a somewhat unusual yet very interesting service. NETworth publishes a regular series of articles by various mutual fund experts, and the **Meet the Experts** page is where you can read their opinions, as well as participate in an ongoing forum where people post questions, reactions, or opinions, just like on a Usenet newsgroup. If you're looking for expert opinions and advice about mutual fund investing, this is the place for you!

Market Outlook. This feature provides articles on the investment markets that are updated weekly. These are typically short, concise stories that cover the state of the markets in a few broad strokes. Past articles are also available by clicking on links right at the bottom of this page:

- **The Forum.** The Forum area on NETworth is an archive of background information on mutual funds and fund investing. If you need an education on mutual funds and terminology, the Forum should be your first stop.

- **The Equities Center.** While primarily oriented toward providing information for mutual fund investors, NETworth also has some nice features for investors who are interested in stocks. Many of the features of the Equities Center are available right from the Center's Web page, while others can be accessed by clicking links on the image map at the top of the page. Currently, NETworth offers stock investors:

- **NETworth Quote Server.** A place to get quick and easy stock quotes and graphs. You can also search for company information here. This feature is not as robust as some of the stock information available from *The Wall Street Journal* or Hoover's, but it is a great place for quick updates and graphs. Graphs can be customized to show prices for different date ranges.

- **Your Personal Portfolio.** This is a great feature for investors in both stocks and mutual funds. You can set up a portfolio with the NETworth site by clicking on the **Personal Portfolio** link on the NETworth home page. To set up your portfolio, simply fill out the form with your stock or fund symbols, as well as your purchase prices. Click on a few option buttons to configure your portfolio, then click on **Submit**. That's it! Now you can get a quick overview of the performance of your entire portfolio in one convenient place.

- **Investor Relations Resource.** This is a directory of the home pages of many publicly listed companies. Either click on a letter in the alphabetical index, or enter a search request in the search text box.

- **Disclosure Incorporat**ed. This link leads to a host of information services offered by Disclosure, Inc. Disclosure makes a tremendous amount of public company information available to the investing public through its extensive database.

- **I/B/E/S Earnings Forecasts.** I/B/E/S provides earnings estimates and forecasts that are widely used in the industry to assess the future prospects of various companies. Having access to accurate earnings estimates can be an invaluable tool for the individual investor.

The Financial Planner. The Financial Planner service offered by NETworth is a center of educational information, worksheets to help you calculate your investment goals and needs, and tips designed to give you investment ideas and advice. This area, like the other main areas offered by NETworth, contains sublinks to other pages of interest. The Financial Planner includes:

- **The Perspective Advisory Company.** This company is a registered investment adviser that offers advice and information for investors on NETworth. This page offers a number of educational documents and articles for investors.

- **American Association of Individual Investors.** The AAII, to which you were introduced in chapter two, maintains its presence here on NETworth. The AAII is dedicated to increasing knowledge among individual investors. It does not make investment recommendations, so opinions expressed here tend to be quite objective. This site is a must for all investors!

- **Fielder Financial Management Limited.** This page is dedicated to providing investors with information about investments that offer tax benefits of various sorts. If you are interested in tax shelters, tax-deferred investments, or tax-free investments, this page can provide you with plenty of information on these topics.

- **Zurich Direct.** A site with information about various types of insurance plans and how to invest in insurance.

The Insider. This is a comprehensive search service that will allow you to find information that NETworth offers on any number of investment-related topics. You can find information about stocks, mutual funds, bonds and interest rates, taxes, commodities and derivatives, and numerous other investments. A great source of information, or a great place to click around on just to see what you'll find!

The NETworth Information Desk. Help and information about the NETworth Web site, how to get around, and how to use various features and services offered.

The Quicken Financial Network. A link to the home page of **Intuit, Inc.,** which provides all sorts of investment information, information about Intuit products, technical support for products, and links to other investment and financial sites.

Although the current offerings for stock and equity investors are not as complete as some other sites, the NETworth Web site offers a breadth of investment information that is virtually unmatched (with the possible exception of *The Wall Street Journal* online). No single site can be all things for all investors, but NETworth certainly tries and comes very close.

Hoover's Online

 If your investment strategy is primarily focused on stocks, and you need to find detailed and up-to-date information about publicly traded companies, **Hoover's Online** should definitely be on your list of favorite places! The amount of data available

here for equity investors is amazing—Hoover's offers a massive database on over 10,000 companies—and everything is well organized and easy to find. Some of the services are free while others are available only by subscription for $9.95 per month. The extra information available for this price may very well be worth considering. To get to Hoover's on the Web, enter: http://www.hoovers.com

Navigating Hoover's Online

 Like many other sites on the Internet, Hoover's offers an image map at the top of the screen that you can click on to get to the various services offered. **Hoover's Online** also provides text links to most of these services right from the home page, if you'd rather not use the image map. Simply scroll down the page to see the links that are available. Services offered by Hoover's, and available by clicking on the appropriate icon on the image map (or on the home page itself) include:

Quick Stock Quotes. Enter a ticker symbol, and click on the **Get a DBC Quote** button to get a stock quote on any company. Simple! This option is available right on the home page. Further down on the home

Welcome to Hoover's Online, where we prove that company information doesn't have to be boring!

Free access to The Corporate Directory is brought to you by E*TRADE:

page is another text box in which you can enter up to seven stock symbols to get quotes and basic earnings information for the stocks you've entered. A great source of quick information about companies!

What's Here. This is Hoover's Online directory and help system. Click on the **What's Here** icon on the image map to get to this area. You'll find a listing of all the services offered by Hoover's Online, as well as information about Hoover's itself.

This is a good place to go the first few times you visit Hoover's Online because it will introduce you to all the features available.

Member's Only. This section contains the services that are available only by subscription. Benefits of subscribing to the service are also listed here. Membership benefits include access to additional, more in-depth company information than is available in the free areas of Hoover's, access to the **Big Buzz** news archives, and

other features not available to nonsubscribers.
Corporate Web Register. This is a very useful service in that it offers links to Web sites for over 2,000 different companies. If you've been trying with no luck to find the Web site for your favorite company, this database may have what you're looking for! The entries are listed alphabetically, with a clickable A to Z directory at the top of the page that will take you right to the group of companies whose names start with the selected letter.

Corporate Directory. This is a huge database of information on over 10,000 companies! The database provides you with information that includes stock prices, a basic company profile, and links to other sites that have information about the selected company. You can search the database by ticker symbol or company name, or by creating a query based on the company's location, industry group, or sales.

Company Profile Database. A subscription-only service, this database offers in-depth analysis and information about selected companies. There are over 2,200 companies profiled in this database, and the list is growing.

Marketplace. Here's where you can order various items of interest to investors, ranging from books and software products to specialized investment newsletters and reports.

Features & Contests. This area provides a listing of news and investment features that Hoover's offers in addition to their regular services. Useful features include **Earnings Report**, a listing of new 10-K and 10-Q reports filed with the Securities and Exchange Commission, and the **Industry Focus**, which

includes regularly updated reports on various industries and the outlook for business in those industries. There are also a number of contests that you can enter, such as the weekly business trivia contest. Some of these contests even offer cash prizes!

Biz Buzz. This is Hoover's news and headlines service. Regular news and information updates about industry and economic happenings are provided here for investors. The news stories tend to be focused on issues and events that are particularly interesting to investors, rather than an overall rehash of all the day's news. Very useful and focused information.

Of course, like many other sites on the Web, Hoover's Online also has links to other investment and information services on the Internet, so you can always find more by simply clicking around and following the links. The offerings available here are continually growing, so check back frequently to keep yourself current on your favorite companies.

The Securities and Exchange Commission (SEC)

 Hoover's Online isn't the only place on the Internet where you can find detailed information on various companies. In fact, much of the information available on Hoover's is directly available from the **Securities and Exchange Commission**'s home page. To get there, enter: http://www.sec.gov/

The SEC is the government agency that is charged with overseeing the various securities markets in America. This agency enforces rules that are designed to keep publicly traded businesses honest in their dealings with shareholders, the press, and other organizations. The SEC also oversees the various stock exchanges and bond markets that actively trade securities and ensures that material information is disclosed to investors.

In order to do this, the SEC requires that publicly listed corporations file quarterly (10-Q) and annual (10-K) reports that detail the nature and the state of the corporation's business. This information is invaluable for investors, because it helps them weed out the truth about a company's

United States Securities & Exchange Commission

SEC

"We are the investor's advocate."
- William O. Douglas, SEC Chairman, 1937-1939

450 5th Street N.W. Washington, D.C. 20549

Current News:

Decision: U.S. SEC vs. Frederick Augustus Moran et al.

EDGAR Phase-in Complete on May 6, 1996

The Joint Regulatory Sales Practice Sweep Report Released

Report of the Task Force on Disclosure Simplification Published

situation. While press releases and broker's recommendations may have nothing but good things to say about a company (even if that company is a quickly sinking ship), the financial reports required by the SEC may present a very different story. This site is a must for anyone who is seriously interested in investing in stocks.

The resources provided for investors on the SEC home page include the following, and they are easily accessible directly from links on the home page:

Current News. This section provides updates and information regarding recent activities of the SEC, including legal actions and settlements, regulatory changes that may affect investors or corporations that are required to file reports with the SEC, and various reports and news articles that relate to the operations of the SEC and how they may affect investors or corporations.

About the SEC. A very interesting and detailed look at the agency, its purpose, and its history. This area also includes synopses of the important regulations that govern the issuance and trading of securities in America, such as the Securities Act of 1933 and the Investment Company Act of 1940.

What Every Investor Should Know. This section is developed and main- tained by the SEC's Office of Investor Education and Assistance. This area provides investors with a great deal of information on how to invest wisely and to avoid securities fraud or other abuses. The articles available here are a great introduction to the securities markets, how they work, and how to avoid being taken advantage of. There are many links to online documents that offer educational information for investors, such as:

- **Invest Wisely.** How to choose a broker, pick an investment, and look out for trouble.

- **Arbitration Procedures.** Important information on resolving disputes against stockbrokers.

EDGAR Database of Corporate Information. This is where you'll find disclosure documents for nearly all publicly listed corporations. EDGAR stands for Electronic Data Gathering, Analysis, and Retrieval system. This system currently contains disclosure information on over 75 percent of publicly traded domestic corporations. In May 1996, the SEC began to require electronic filing of documents for all publicly traded companies, so the amount of information available on this database will continue to increase. Although not all documents required by the SEC are going to be available through EDGAR, the most important documents for investors, the 10-K and 10-Q reports, will.

The feature of the EDGAR system that will be of most interest to investors is the Search feature, which allows you to find disclosure documents on any number of companies.

Simply click on the **Search the EDGAR Database** link on the EDGAR Web page, and you'll be presented with a search screen that allows you to search for information about companies. This page offers helpful instructions to make your searches more successful.

SEC News Digests and Public Statements. This area contains an archive of news about the SEC, other reports about the agency, press releases, speeches by SEC officials, Congressional testimony, special studies, and the SEC's annual report.

Current SEC Rule Making: Proposals and Final Rules. Information about legislation that the SEC has proposed or has agreed upon. This area is very interesting in that you can see the rule-making process in action. Occasionally, the SEC even invites public commentary on proposals!

SEC Enforcement Actions. An archive of various SEC actions against corporations and/or individuals. There are some items of interest here, but many of the actions are taken against companies that have failed to file required reports.

About this Site and FAQ. Just what it sounds like! Help and information about navigating the SEC's Web site, and a page of Frequently Asked Questions about the SEC's site.

Other Sites of Interest. This link takes you to a page that lists a number of other interesting government sites, such as

- The White House
- FinanceNet
- FedWorld
- U.S. House of Representatives

The **FinanceNet** link may be of interest to investors in that it contains information on Treasury operations and various other aspects of the financial operations of the federal government. It also contains information about the state of the national economy and the national debt. If you're interested in purchasing government assets that are on sale to the public, you can do that here too!

The Securities and Exchange Commission provides an invaluable service for investors. If it weren't for the regulatory controls placed on the markets by the SEC, the amount of securities fraud and abuses would probably get out of hand very quickly. This Web site should be required reading for all cyberinvestors. The educational materials available here are excellent, and the corporate reports and filings will help you see clearly through any smoke that a company or investment relations firm may be trying to blow over the truth.

Silicon Investor

 If you believe that high-tech investments are an important part of your portfolio, then the **Silicon Investor** Web site should be at the top of your list of favorite places. To get to Silicon Investor, enter: http://www.techstocks.com/

The service is available for no charge, but you must be registered to participate in the interactive forums. To do so, simply click on the **Register** link on the Silicon Investor home page, then fill out the form online, and click on the **Register Me!** button.

Some of the features that can be accessed by the home page include:

Charts. Get charts on stock prices and trading volumes for your favorite technology stocks. You can customize the time frame for the chart, create a printable version of the chart to download, get a profile of the company, or post mes-

sages to the discussion forum on the selected stock.

StockTalk. An interactive forum, similar to Usenet or AOL's discussion forums, where you can create topics for discussions.

Discussion topics are organized by categories such as:

- Miscellaneous
- Computers
- Software
- Communications
- Semiconductors

Within each group, postings are in alphabetical order so you can quickly locate a particular thread that may be of interest to you. You'll often run into people here who are experts in various fields of technology, so there's plenty to learn. If you are a technowizard, your input will most certainly be appreciated here.

Groups. This feature of Silicon Investor allows you to create customized groups of stocks that you may be interested in following. There are also predefined stock groups that

are categorized by technology sector in the same topic listings as the StockTalk area. These groups allow you to get quick information on up to 30 different stocks per group, arranged in a table-style format. The stock groups that you create (or view, if you're using pre-defined groups) can be viewed in different formats, including:

- **Quotes.**
  Basic quote information for the stock group, including high, low, and closing prices, daily volume, and percentage change for the stock prices listed.

- **Financials.**
  Includes date of the company's next quarter-end period, annual revenues, net income, and total number of outstanding shares. This view also shows the current share price, the price/sales ratio, and the market capitalization of the company.

- **Comp Charts.**
  Allows you to select up to seven of the stocks in the current group to be used in the creation of a custom comparison chart. Simply click on a check box next to the stocks you want included in your chart, then click on the **Generate Chart** button at the bottom of the page. You can

customize the time frame used for the chart, or create a printable version for downloading.

- **More Info.**
  This feature gives you access to additional information about the companies in your group. You can click on a link to the Silicon Investor's own company profile for any of the stocks in the group, or you can click on a link to that company's home page.

Spotlight. This link takes you to a page that features stocks that fit certain criteria. The links available in the Spotlight are:

- **Feature.**
  This section includes feature articles by various financial experts, daily selections of stocks that appear to have good prospects, and other selected information. The Feature section changes monthly.

- **Big Movers.**
  Displays two daily top ten lists: the top stocks in upward price movement for the day, and the top stocks in downward price movement for the day. Each company is listed as a link to its Silicon Investor profile.

- **Volume.**
  Again, two top ten lists:

the top ten volume leaders (in terms of shares traded) for the day, and the top ten volume percentage leaders, displayed as links to profile pages.

- **Hot Charts.**
  Links to a wide variety of comparative stock charts, from a comparison of different semiconductor companies to comparisons of various networking companies. You can suggest comparison charts to Silicon Investor by clicking on an e-mail link to their Webmaster. If they like your idea, it may appear in this list!

- **Indexes.**
  Charts and information about various technology-oriented indexes, plus links to explanations and information about the indexes and what they track.

Profiles. This area is where Silicon Investor provides you with in-depth company information about the various stocks they cover. At the top of this page, you'll see a very simple image map displaying the letters A through Z. Click on a letter, and you'll be taken to a group of companies that start with that letter. Click on the company's name, and you'll be taken to a detailed profile of that company, which includes information about the company's business focus, links to StockTalk discussion topics about the company, press releases and financial information from the company, and links to that company's home page.

Quotes. Quick and simple quotes. Enter a symbol, select a few options, click on **Submit,** and you'll have your 15-minute delayed quote in seconds! You can also create a personal portfolio of up to seven stocks here. This feature does not currently allow you to enter your number of shares and purchase price, but only lists the stocks and their pricing information.

Bull/Bear Sentiment Survey. See how other silicon investors feel about the current state of the market! You can add your own opinions to this ongoing survey or view current results of the survey. Occasionally there are other surveys available here as well, if you like to participate in these sorts of things!

Calendar. This is a very interesting feature that is currently unique to the Silicon Investor site. The **Interactive Calendar** displays upcoming events of

importance for investors, such as the release dates for various economic indicators (e.g., the book-to-bill ratio, which is a key indicator for semiconductor stocks), expected release dates for corporate earnings, any new initial public offerings (IPOs) that may be taking place, and other important dates and times.

You can make entries to this calendar if you have information that would be useful to other members of the site. A great source of data on upcoming events!

Trading Stocks on the World Wide Web

 As on America Online, the rest of the World Wide Web is becoming a place where you can buy and sell investments! Most trading sites require a browser that can support this feature. Be aware that the browser in AOL version 2.5 does not yet support secure transactions. But the feature should be available in the next release of its software. Here are some sites that currently offer stock and/or mutual fund trading capabilities.

PAWWS Financial Network

 The PAWWS Financial Network is a complete

investors' resource, even without the ability to trade online. However, with this added capability, the site becomes a complete center for personal financial management. To get there enter: http://pawws.secapl.com/

The distinguishing feature of PAWWS is not that you can conduct financial transactions online, or even that the site offers a lot of good investment information. What's unique about PAWWS is that it is a network of investment resources, offering you "one-stop shopping" for information and transactions that are of great value to investors. For example, while most sites that trade online require that you have an account with their service, PAWWS allows you to trade with a number of different online brokerage services right from the PAWWS home page. The service offered by PAWWS is free, but you must register in order to open an account with one of the service providers listed on its network.

Integrated Financial Products

 The first section of the PAWWS home page is the **Integrated Financial Products,** which offers the following links:

- **Brokerage Services.** This page provides information about and links to get to the various Affiliate Brokers of the PAWWS Financial Network. These brokerages offer a number of services, from portfolio accounting to online trading. In order to conduct transactions online with one of these firms, you'll need to open an account with them first. Click on the link to any of the Affiliate Brokers to find information about how to open an account.

- **Portfolio Accounting.** PAWWS offers a large selection of services to track and maintain your portfolio. Some of the services are available to you for free if you have an account with one of the Affiliate Brokers of the network. Otherwise, you'll have to pay a subscription fee to use the Portfolio Accounting feature.

- **Mutual Funds/Portfolio Management.** This link takes you to the Gabelli Asset Management Company's home page. This site has a great deal of information for mutual fund investors.

- **News & Commentary.** This is a link to DTN Wall Street services. This information service offers a large number of

investor-oriented news services which are available by subscription only.

- **Market Analysis.** This is a link to the **Griffin Financial Services** Web site. This page provides a number of news and information services for investors, some of which are available free to PAWWS Network members; others are available only by subscription.

- **Technical Analysis**. This link takes you to the Stock Market Index Inc. (SMI) home page. This page offers useful information about the markets, as well as technical analysis of trends, a market screen to allow you to find potentially good investments, a weekly market report, and access to TACTIX™, a proprietary portfolio strategy tool for investors.

- **Real Time/Delayed Pricing.** PAWWS offers stock and fund pricing services by subscription. Real-time quotes are available for $50 per month. This service may be of great value to you if you are interested in tracking all trading activity during the course of a trading day.

- **Fundamental Data.** This link takes you to

the home page of **Ford Investor Services, Inc.** Ford offers in-depth stock research to subscribers. If you are in need of detailed research on potential investments, you may want to consider subscribing to one of Ford's research services.

- **Financial Publications.** The PAWWS network provides access to **MF Information Services** and **Money Talks** (a publication of PR Newswire). These online newsletters offer the investor a great deal of information about stocks, mutual funds, and other investments. MF Information Services is a free resource available to PAWWS members that offers mutual fund information as well as information about other financial newsletters. *Money Talks* is an electronic magazine designed to help the individual investor make informed investment decisions based on a broad range of information. This site provides investors with in-depth articles, research, and information about numerous investment topics.

More Information. The second major section of the

CUSTOMER LOG ON

Visitor Center
Register for free Stock Quotes or play our Stock Market Game.

Trading Demo
Find out what it's like to trade with E*TRADE.

The E*TRADE Advantage
Superior

Welcome to the Smarter Way to Trade.

E*TRADE offers one of the lowest and simplest commission structures available (only **$14.95** for market orders of Listed securities) and the most efficient, fully-automated stock and option trading system on the Web.

Customers can log on here (please note, our secure server requires Netscape Navigator version 1.2 or higher). Visitors, take a quick

---

PAWWS home page is called **More Information**, which is where you can find additional help and resources about the PAWWS network itself. Some of the links available here are:

- **Complete Price List.** A listing of prices for all the various subscription services offered by PAWWS and the Affiliated Brokers. This page also has a listing of all the free services that are available on PAWWS, so you may want to start exploring here if you don't have subscriptions to some of the paid services.

- **Learn More about the PAWWS Financial Network.** This page has information about PAWWS itself, including employment opportunities, a history of the service, press releases, and other information.

- **Frequently Asked Questions (FAQs).** Links to FAQs about the services offered by PAWWS and its affiliates.

- **About Your Privacy.** Brief information about security issues on the Internet and how to use secure browsers to conduct online transactions.

If you're looking for commercial brokerage services, news services, or other commercial resources for investors, PAWWS is a great place to compare and contrast services.

Ceres Securities

 Ceres Securities is a brokerage firm that offers inexpensive transaction fees for all kinds of stock-related transactions. With Ceres, you can trade stocks, open short positions on stocks, and buy, sell, or write options. This is a commercial service that prides itself on providing "executions only" service to self-sufficient investors. If you are confident in your own

Real-Time Trading and Research Information

Welcome to the <u>Lombard Institutional Brokerage</u> Real-Time Trading and Research Information Center. Our philosophy is simple: 'Through the use of cutting edge technology, we are dedicated to providing our customers in the Internet community with a wide variety of investment options, enhanced investment tools and an unparalleled commitment to customer service...'

 *(1/24/96)* Check out the **new features** at Lombard or a brief demonstration of the site.

ability to manage your investments and want a broker who will place orders for you without trying to sell you something or offer you investment advice, Ceres Securities may be right for you. To get to the Ceres home page, enter: http://www.ceres.com/

Ceres Securities is proud that it actually offers very little information to investors. Its primary purpose is to offer investors who have Ceres accounts the opportunity to track their portfolios, place orders, and get quick stock quotes, although daily market commentaries from Andrew Tobias are provided in addition to the primary portfolio management features of the site.

This is a no-frills service center for the independent investor, and the cost per transaction justifies the service as a very attractive place for investors to trade stocks and options. You'll need to open an account with Ceres to begin conducting transactions, of course, but once you've done that you'll be able to trade stocks quickly and easily from this Web site.

E*Trade

 E*Trade, like Ceres Securities, offers a bare-bones home page that is oriented primarily to its account holders. If you open an account with E*Trade, you can get an online overview of your portfolio and place trades for securities. Even if you don't have an account, you can get quick stock quotes here. To get to E*Trade, enter: http://www.etrade.com/

One interesting feature of the E*Trade site is its **Stock Market Game.** This is a good way for newer investors to get a little practice before actually putting real money on the line! The game area offers the following features:

- You can trade stocks or stocks and options using real market prices.

Welcome from Charles Schwab.

- You start with a portfolio of $100,000 in "game money," and portfolio and transaction records are updated automatically.

- The top ten players are posted daily on the Web site.

- A new game starts every month.

E*Trade is a very competitively priced trading service that offers good executions without all the frills of a full-service brokerage account. This is another great option for the self-reliant investor.

Lombard Institutional Brokerage

 Lombard is another site that offers discounted trading on the Web. To get to Lombard's home page, enter: http://www.lombard.com/ Lombard offers online trading for account holders, as well as the **Lombard Investment Center,** where active account holders can manage their portfolios and get access to additional information. However, Lombard also offers the **Public Access Center** for individuals who are not currently Lombard account holders.

To use the Public Access Center, you'll first need to register with Lombard by clicking on the **Free Registration Desk** link on the **Lombard** home page. Once you've registered, you'll have access to stock quotes, graphs, and research links to a number of other investment-oriented Internet sites, such as the **SEC** home page and **Hoover's Company Information.** Lombard also offers a number of full-service brokerage options, such as mutual fund investment, personal money management services, and insurance services. If you're looking for a brokerage service that allows you to trade online, but also offers a wider variety of services than some of the deep-discount firms such as Ceres or E*Trade, you may want to consider opening an account with Lombard.

Schwab Online

 One of the most well-known discount brokerages, Charles Schwab, now has a presence on the Web called **e.Schwab**. To get to this site, enter: http://www.schwab.com/

The Schwab investment site, like Lombard, offers more services to investors than some of the other deep discount services on the Web. Schwab offers account holders the ability to trade stocks and mutual fund shares, and to get access to account information and portfolios. Non-account holders can get access to information resources such as Schwab's investment library. (Articles can be sent to you by regular mail.) Schwab also provides customized software to account holders that allows you to track your investments, maintain portfolios, and conduct online transactions.

The Closing Bell

 One of the best mailing lists avail-able to investors is the Closing Bell service offered by **Mercury Mail, Inc.** The Closing Bell mailing list is a subscription-only service that allows you to create a custom information service that is tailored to your needs. Mercury Mail will let you have a free limited-time trial subscription so you can check out the service before actually subscribing. To sign up for a free trial, enter: http://www.merc.com/cbell2.html

Closing Bell allows you to create a completely customized investment information service that will be e-mailed to you each day at the close of the major stock exchanges. When you sign up, you will be taken to a Web page that lets you enter up to 30 stock symbols that the service will track for you. After your request for a subscription has been accepted, you'll start receiving daily updates by e-mail of the closing prices of your selected stocks, including the high price, low price, and trading volume for the day. You'll also get a synopsis of any news stories that may have been released that day in relation to any of the stocks you are tracking.

This is a great service if you want to keep abreast of your investments on a daily basis, but aren't able or willing to log in to different services every day to find the information. The Closing Bell will act as an information agent for you, in that it will send you all this information automatically, right to your e-mail in-box.

Keeping Up with What's Available

 Now that you've gotten started exploring investment opportunities in cyberspace, you've probably already discovered that there are more resources available than any single book could possibly cover. As you continue traveling, you'll find that your searches will become more productive and enjoyable if you keep in mind these few principles:

- **The Internet is always changing.** To keep up with what's new, you've got to surf on a regular basis. If a site changes or disappears, just remember that there are always other interesting places to visit, and new sites will continue to appear.

- **Many of the investment-related sites on the Internet have similiar types of information.** You'll need to explore and find what suits you best. **Book-mark** pages that you really like, or add them to your list of **Favorite Places.** You don't have to visit every single site on the Web to find what you need.

- **Don't stop looking!** Most Web sites have links to other Web sites, and so on. Have no fear! Click on any link that attracts your attention. If something turns out to be a dead-end or requires you to be a sub-scriber (and you don't want to be), just click on the **BACK** button on your Web browser to return to previous sites.

- **And most important, don't ignore traditional sources of investment information.** Hundreds of newsletters, maga-zines, and services are available out there, and they aren't all on the Internet (yet!). A well-balanced investment approach should take into consideration everything that might be of use, whether in cyberspace or in the real world. Just remember to always do your home-work before you cast your money forth!

SEARCHING OTHER COMMERCIAL SERVICES

WHILE AMERICA
ONLINE MAY BE
THE MOST POPU-
LAR ONLINE SER-
VICE TODAY,
and the Internet itself is
unparalleled in the amount
of information it offers,
there are a number of other
online services that you
might want to explore,
each with significant offerings for investors. Each
service has its own particular forums and features
and, like America Online,
each also provides access
to the Internet, the mother
of all networks. The choices you make when decid-
ing to use any of these services depend on the type
of material you're looking
for, the costs involved, and
how comfortable you feel
about the service's ability
to interface effectively. In
short, the differences
between the various online
services may or may not be
that significant in the long
run, but it is your personal
preference, more than anything else, that should dic-
tate where you spend your
online dollars and time.

While not quite as popular
as America Online, there
are three other online services which boast member-
ships in the millions of
subscribers: **CompuServe,
The Microsoft Network,**

and **Prodigy.** Each provides a great deal of information that can help you
make investing decisions,
research possible invest-
ment opportunities, and
conduct transactions
online. Best of all, you can
join any of these services
and get a free trial period
which gives you a chance
to decide whether you
want to become a member
for the longer term.

Joining any of these ser-
vices is easy, very much
like signing up with
America Online. Prodigy
and CompuServe software
is often "bundled" with
Internet or computer mag-
azines, or it's mailed
directly to you, whereas
The Microsoft Network is
actually included with the
Windows 95 installation
software. Run the installation program according to

the instructions, then continue to follow the steps
provided by the software
as it installs. To load The
Microsoft Network (if your
Windows 95 installation
did not already create a
Microsoft Network icon on
your desktop):

• Press the **Start** button.

• Click on **Settings.**

• Click on **Control Panel.**

• Double-click on the
  Add/Remove Programs
  icon.

• Click on the **Windows
  Setup** tab.

• Select **The Microsoft
  Network** from the list of
  options and click on
  OK.

Each of these services has
an 800 or local number that
you can call during the initial installation. Once

you're online, you select telephone numbers to access the service. If you have trouble, you can contact the technical support people at the service who will be happy to walk you through any problems you may experience. Or, if you already have an Internet connection you can visit any of those respective Websites to get information. You can request the software to access the service from these numbers and Web sites as well, with the exception of The Microsoft Network software, which is included as part of Windows 95. The contacts for each service are:

- **CompuServe**

  (800) 848-8199

  http://www.compuserve.com

- **The Microsoft Network**

  (800) 386-5550

  (206) 882-8080

  http://www.msn.com

- **Prodigy**

  (800) 776-3449

  http://www.prodigy.com

CompuServe

 CompuServe is one of the oldest and most complete online services available today. Although it has fewer members than America Online, the numbers are very close, and it may actually provide a greater overall quantity of services than America Online. CompuServe is particularly strong in the area of technical information for computer users, but its financial offerings are also quite extensive, and are certainly competitive to what's available on America Online. However, one drawback of CompuServe is that currently many of the more in-depth financial services can only be accessed for an additional surcharge to your normal billing rate. While the service is meticulous about informing you when you are entering an additional charge area, you may be unpleasantly surprised when you get the bill if you've spent a good deal of time doing extensive online research.

The CompuServe interface is not quite as attractive as America Online's, but the services are relatively easy to navigate, and you'll be able to find a great deal of useful investment information quickly. The first thing you'll notice when you log on to CompuServe is the **Explore Services** screen. If you click on the **Finance** button here, you'll be taken to CompuServe's primary source of financial and investment information, the **Money Personal Finance Center.** This screen offers you a host of options for exploring financial and investment topics, from stock quotes and portfolios to financial and business news. You'll also find CompuServe's investment forums here, which are similar to America Online's discus-

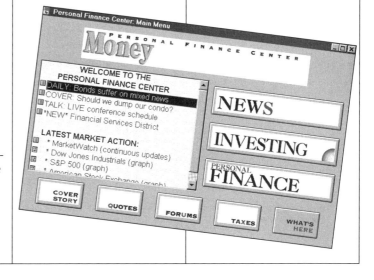

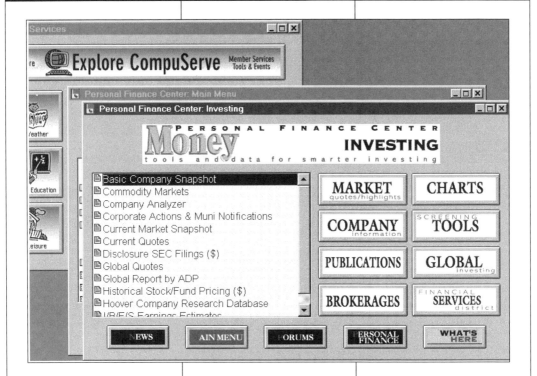

sion and Usenet news-groups. These forums provide a place for investors to gather and discuss all sorts of topics relating to personal finance.

You can use The Personal Finance Center as your base of operations if you are a CompuServe user looking for investment and financial information. On the left hand side of the screen you'll see a list of the most current news and information relating to the financial and business markets. You can easily keep up with the latest news and information by checking in to this area on a regular basis. The large buttons on the right hand side of the screen offer you access to three key financial areas of CompuServe:

News. Provides access to news services such as:

- Reuters Business Headlines
- Time News Center
- Money Daily
- Business Wire
- *USA Today*
- Fortune Daily
- PR Newswire
- Personalized News

Investing. This area provides a central location for in-depth investment research and information. Some of the features here include:

- Market Quotes/ Highlights
- Publications
- Screening Tools
- Global Investing
- Financial Services District

Personal Finance. This area offers investment advice, discussions, and other information oriented toward the individual or family investor. The features here include:

- Savings rates (borrowing and credit)

- Answers (Budget Doctor)
- Publications
- One Family's Finances
- Taxes
- Save On…
- Your Goals
- Money

Each of these topics is actually a button that will take you to additional screens that provide access to even more in-depth information or other services that may prove to be invaluable to active investors.

CompuServe also offers you the ability to get to a particular area of its service by using a **GO** word, which functions like AOL's **Keywords.** Once you've learned the GO words that will take you to topics of interest, you simply click on the GO button on your toolbar (which looks like a street light on green!) and enter the GO word to take you to your destination. For example, to get to The Personal Finance Center, you can use the GO word "FINANCE." Another CompuServe GO word that you'll find very useful is "INVEST." This will take you to a menu that lists a series of investment services available on Compuserve. Some of these services include:

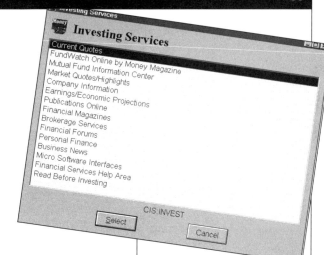

- Market Quotes/Highlights
- Company Information
- Financial Forums
- Personal Finance
- Business News

Some of the other CompuServe GO words you'll want to remember:

- BUSDB. Business Database Plus
- ANALYZER. Company Analyzer
- BASCOMPANY. Company Snapshot
- CQUOTE. Current Stock Quotes
- DISCLOSURE . Disclosure Inc. (SEC documents)
- DIVIDENDS. Information on stock splits and dividends
- FORBES. Forbes Magazine Online

- FORTUNE. Fortune Magazine Online
- INVFORUM. The Investors' Forum
- MARKET. Market Highlights
- ENS. Personalized News Services
- SYMBOLS. Stock quote symbol lookup

In addition to the regular forums and services, CompuServe has a number of services that investors can customize to help find and track information. Here are three.

Portfolio

 This feature enables you to set up your own personal portfolio of investment information and stocks. You can easily keep track of the value of your portfolio by taking advantage of this feature. You'll need to set up the stocks that you want to track, along with the number of shares you've purchased and the purchase price. Then, whenever you visit this area you'll be able to get a valuation of your entire portfolio. Use the GO word "PORTFOLIO" to get to this feature.

Personalized News Service

 Here you can get immediate information from various news services on search criteria that you enter. You can also get news updates on a list of companies by entering their stock symbols. When you save this personalized configuration, CompuServe will automatically update your news folder with stories relating to the companies you've chosen to track. To get here, use the GO word "**ENS**."

Stock Quotes

 CompuServe actually offers two different ways to get stock quote updates. One way is to use the Keyword "**CQUOTE**" to get to a terminal emulation screen in which you can get quotes one at a time. The other way is to use the default toolbar option for quotes. On the toolbar that is set up when you installed

CompuServe, you'll find a button with a little ticker symbol and price, along with the word "QUOTES." If you click on this button, you'll get to a screen from

which you can get stock quotes for a personalized list of symbols, and charts of stock prices over time. To add a symbol to your list, simply click on the **ADD** button then enter the ticker symbol. To get a quote, you can select items from the list and click on "Get", or you can click on "Get All" to get an update of all the stocks in your list.

CompuServe is a comprehensive online service that rivals any other in terms of the depth and breadth of its coverage of financial and investment topics. You can spend hours here exploring the various financial offerings without even beginning to exhaust the vast resources available. And, to top it all off, CompuServe also offers direct access to the World Wide Web so you can jump from the Net to CompuServe and back again when you do your research. This service is certainly worth exploring if you are interested in

expanding your online explorations into new territory.

Prodigy

 Prodigy is another online service that has been around for a number of years. This was one of the biggest, most successful services at the beginning of the "online era" (mid-1980s), but it has lost much of its luster to competitors like AOL and CompuServe. The first thing you'll notice when you log on to Prodigy is its somewhat antiquated user interface. Prodigy has not done nearly as well as America Online, CompuServe, or The Microsoft Network in updating its interface and making it attractive and user-friendly, and sometimes you'll feel like you're a bit behind the times while cyberwandering around its world.

Nonetheless, the content on Prodigy is quite good, and if you're looking for investment information there's no question that you'll find a lot here that's of value.

Each time you log on to Prodigy, you'll be offered a choice of four initial destinations :

• Highlights

• Web Browser

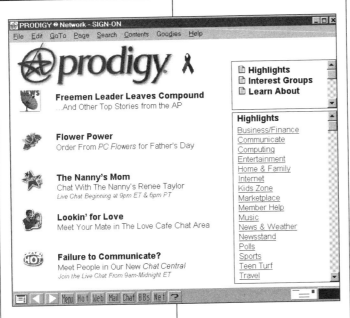

- Hot List
- Member Help Center

The screen you see here is the **Highlights** screen, which is the default option when you first sign on to the network. The Highlights screen has a listing of new features and news on the left hand side of the screen, and on the right you'll see a list of services and forums that are regularly available. Currently, the first item on the right-hand list is the Business/Finance selection, which takes you to the **Prodigy Business & Finance** screen.

Business & Finance Area

 The Business & Finance area is the best place to start exploring Prodigy for investment and financial information. This screen is nicely arranged and provides a great deal of information in a small amount of space. Across the top you'll find updates on the major market indexes such as the Dow Jones Industrial Average or the Nasdaq Composite. Just below this area and on the left hand side of the screen you can get information and news headlines at-a-glance. If you double-

click on any of these entries you'll be taken to the full text of that news item. And below the headlines area on the same screen you'll see a regularly updated list of special topics and scheduled discussions that are taking place online. On the right hand side of the **Business & Finance** screen you'll see a menu of Prodigy's main financial and business offerings. Simply click on any of these items and you'll get right to the area you are interested in.

Prodigy, like all the other online services, offers the ability to jump to any forum or area of the service by using a Keyword or Jump word. To access this feature on Prodigy:

- Click on **Go To** on the main menu at the top of the screen.
- Click on **Jump To** in the drop-down menu.

- Enter the **Jump** word that you want to use.
- Click on **OK.**

Prodigy also offers the option of using a keyboard command to access the Jump screen. To Jump quickly to another area, you can press the **CTRL-J** key combination. For example, to get directly to the Business & Finance area, you can use the Jump word "Finance." If you enter either the Jump word "Investing" or "Personal Finance" you'll be taken to menus listing all the available investment-related areas on the Prodigy network. Some of the more interesting Jump words you can use to find investment topics include:

- Boyd on Investments
- Company News
- Company Reports
- CR Investments
- Financial Services
- Fund at a Glance
- Investor's Glossary
- Markets & Economy
- Money Talk
- Stock at a Glance
- PCFN (PC Financial Network)

Of course, as you work your way through Prodigy's various financial offerings, you'll start to discover some features that you really like and that you'll want to return to on a regular basis. Like AOL's "Favorite Places" feature, Prodigy offers the "**Hot List**" where you can store the Jump words for your favorite services. To access the Prodigy Hot List:

- Click on **Go To** from the main menu.
- Click on **Hot List** from the next menu that appears.

Or, if you want a shortcut key to get to the Hot List, simply press the F3 function key on your keyboard.

One of Prodigy's best features for investors is the **Investment Center,** which is accessible by using the Jump word **Investment Center.** The Investment Center can serve as your central point of reference while you're online with Prodigy simply because it offers the most investment information and links to other investment areas. If you get lost while exploring Prodigy, you can always press CTRL-J to Jump back to the Investment Center.

This feature offers a number of interactive services that can help investors track information and portfolios from a central location. When you first arrive at the Investment Center, you'll be greeted with updates of many of the major market indexes, provided by Reuters WorldQuote. You'll also notice that the Investment Center opens in a separate window from the main Prodigy interface. This window has its own toolbar and menus that allow you to navigate easily among a number of interesting services.

The default toolbar offers easy access to the following services:

- **Quote Check.** Gets you a quick update on the vital statistics for any stock or mutual fund by ticker symbol.

- **Quote Track.** A very useful feature that is similar to Compu-Serve's **Portfolio.** Here you can enter a list of ticker symbols and your purchase price and share amount information. The Quote Track will automatically be updated and will keep track of the value of your investment portfolio.

- **Markets at a Glance.** This is the screen that you first see when you enter the Investment Center. It provides index information and market updates.

- **Company News.** Enter a ticker symbol and

you'll be able to get a quick update on any recent news or information about a company.

- **Online Brokerage.** This button will Jump you to the PC Financial Network (PCFN) screen where you can conduct transactions online.

- **Business & Finance Web Pages.** This will take you to Prodigy's Business and Finance Web site. Here you'll find links to many other investment related Web sites.

All these features, plus a number of others are also available from the **Go To** menu of the Investment Center.

While Prodigy may lack some of the graphics and sophistication of a service like America Online, the information available on the network makes it a serious contender for the loyalty of online information surfers. Prodigy offers a wealth of investment information and services for the individual investor, all of which are easy to use and quite complete in their coverage.

The Microsoft Network

 The Microsoft Network (MSN) is the new kid on the block in the online services

neighborhood. It was first made available in the second half of 1995, and although it is a comparatively recent arrival, Microsoft has done a great job of providing a comprehensive information service for investors in quite a short period of time. The Microsoft Network currently can only be accessed by users of the Windows 95 operating system, although MSN is also accessible on the World Wide Web at http://www.msn.com. If you like the Windows 95

interface, you'll love MSN. The transition to the network is so smooth it will probably feel like you're working in a computer application, although screens usually appear more slowly when you're online. Microsoft has integrated the service into Windows 95 so well that it appears to be a part of the operating system. This is convenient because if you already know how to use Windows 95, you won't have to learn a new interface to explore the network.

When you sign on to MSN, you'll see the **MSN Central** screen which is your "launching pad" into the services of The Microsoft Network. From MSN Central, you can either click on the **MSN Today** icon, or the **Categories** icon to access information about finance and investing.

MSN Today usually appears by default in a typical installation of the service, although you can disable this so that only MSN Central appears. The MSN Today screen provides an overview of what's new and interesting on The Microsoft Network, and also displays information about current happenings on the service.

As you can see, the screen is arranged with a variety of "tabs" that you can click on to get to different subject areas. Click on the **Business & Finance** tab and MSN will display a listing of the features available for investors. In the middle of the screen you'll see a number of large icons which are links to other investment services on the network. At the bottom of the screen, MSN provides a list of upcoming Business & Finance Chats that are taking place that day. On the right hand side of the screen you'll see a list with a scroll bar that you can go through to find MSN's other investment and business services. Click on any of these items and you'll go right to the forum you need.

The other way to find investment information on The Microsoft Network is to click on the large **Categories** icon on the MSN Central screen. This icon will take you to another screen with a listing of the general subject areas that are available. If you click on the **Information & Services** icon, you'll get deeper into the MSN hierarchy of services where you'll find the **Business & Finance** icon (or folder, depending on how you have your Windows 95 interface set up). If you double-click on the Business & Finance icon, you'll get to MSN's investment information headquarters.

The Business & Finance Area

 This area of MSN offers icons (or folders!) that will let you explore all the investment-oriented areas of the network. Some of the items for investors include:

- Business & Finance Info Center

- MSN Business & Finance Guidebook

- Capital Idea Exchange (chat)

- Business & Finance Directory

- Business News & Reference

- Investing

- Personal Finance

- International Trade

- MSN Stock Quotes

Like the other online services, The Microsoft Network offers a quick way to navigate through its services with the **Go To** command, which is available from any menu on any MSN screen. To access this feature, simply click on **Edit**, then **Go To** from the menu. Enter a GO word and you'll get right to where you want to go. To find GO words that you can use on MSN, you can double-click on the **Business & Finance Directory** which is in the Business & Finance folder on the network.

This directory allows you to look for any topic alphabetically by clicking on icons or folders that are labeled by alphabetical groups. So, for example, you could click on the folder labeled "A - E"

or the folder labeled "F - J" to find items whose titles begin with those letters. Or, you can use the **A - Z Index** to find a comprehensive listing of topics available on MSN. Some of the GO words for investment related services on MSN are:

- **Edge.** Thompson Market Edge

- **Schwab.** Schwab Online

- **Investinfo.** Investor Information Forum

- **Hoovers.** Hoover's Business Resources

- **Disclosure.** Disclosure, Inc.

- **Bonds.** Bonds Online

- **Investing.** The Investing Forum

- **Personal Finance.** The Personal Finance Forum

The Microsoft Network also makes it easy for you to find the GO words for forums you are exploring, and to save them in a folder of your **Favorite Places.** If you are in a forum or area on MSN and you want to know what the GO

word is to get to that area, simply click on an empty area of that forum's window with your right mouse button, then click on **Properties** from the pop-up menu that appears. The GO word will be listed along with some of the other properties of the area you are exploring. If you want to quickly add the area to your Favorite Places list, you can either click on **File** from the main menu, then **Add to Favorite Places** from the drop-down menu that appears, or you can click on the Add to Favorite Places icon on the toolbar at the top of the screen.

The Microsoft Network will probably seem like a natural extension of your operating environment. You can use the Find function (**CTRL-F** or **Edit, Find** from the menu) to find information in any part of the network, and you can create shortcuts on your desktop or in folders for quick access to MSN services. The Microsoft Network also provides direct access to the Internet, so you won't be missing out on the vast resources available on the Web and Usenet. MSN is a comprehensive information resource for investors that can provide all the tools you need to be a success in the marketplace.

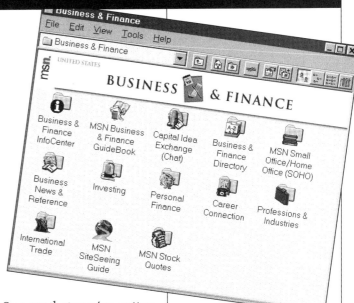

So now that you've gotten a glimpse of some of the resources available to you online, what are you waiting for? By exploring the Web and the other electronic resources you can enhance your investing prowess and get all the information you need to be a successful investor. If you've read this book without logging on, you're missing out on a great deal of useful information that could mean the difference between successful investing and mediocre returns.

So, get yourself a modem, open an account with one of the online service providers discussed in this book, and get wired. You've got nothing to lose and the world to gain, so good luck and good investing!

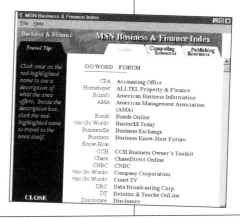

Appendix

Alphabetical List of Investment-Related Web Sites, Newsgroups, and Mutual Fund Sites

CAN'T REMEM-
BER THE URL
FOR A SITE YOU
want to revisit? Here's an
alphabetical list of all the
Web sites (and URLs) men-
tioned in *Point & Click
Investor*, and some others
you might find useful:

Alta Vista
http://www.altavista.
digital.com

**The American Association
of Individual Investors
(AAII)**
http://www.aaii.org

American Stock Report
http://www.awod.com/
gallery/business/asr

Bank Rate Monitor
http://www.bankrate.com

Briefing
http://www.briefing.com

**BulletProof Investor's
WebPage**
http://www.bulletproof.
com

Ceres Securities
http://www.ceres.com/

The Closing Bell
http://www.merc.com/
cbell2.html

**The Conscious Investing
Home Page**
http://investing.com

**Doug Gerlach's Invest-O-
Rama**
http://www.investorama.
com

e.Schwab
http://www.schwab.com/

E*Trade
http://www.etrade.com/

Excite
http://www.excite.com

FAQ Lists for Investors
http://www.smartpages.
com/faqs/
investment-faq/top.html

**Fidelity Online Investor
Center**
http://www.fid-inv.com

The Financial Corner
http://www.
familyinternet.com/fin/
findir.htm

The Financial Data Finder
http://www.cob.ohio-
state.edu/dept/fin/
osudata.htm

Financial Resource Guide
http://www.libertynet.
org/~beausang

Findex - Financial Search
http://www.findex.com/
cgi-bin/findex_search_
markup

Goldman Sachs
http://www.gs.com

Holt Report Index
http://metro.turnpike.
net/holt/index.html

Hoover's Online
http://www.hoovers.
com/

Infoseek NetSearch
http://www.infoseek.com

Inside Wallstreet
http://www.
insidewallstreet.com

**The Insurance Yellow
Pages**
http://www.lifecom.
com

Inter-Links Internet Information Service
http://www.nova.edu/Inter-Links/

Internal Revenue Service
http://www.irs.ustreas.gov/

Investor's Edge
http://www.irnet.com

Investor's FTP site
ftp://dg-rtp.dg.com:/pub/misc.invest

InvestorWEB
http://www.investorweb.com

J.P. Morgan Risk Metrics
http://www.jpmorgan.com/MarketDataInd/RiskMetrics/RiskMetrics.html

Laughinstocks
http://home.gwp.com/wmartin/index.html

Lombard Institutional Brokerage
http://www.lombard.com/

Lycos
http://www.lycos.com

Merrill Lynch
http://www.ml.com

The Microsoft Network
http://www.msn.com

Money Magazine Personal Finance Center
http://www.pathfinder.com/money

The Money Pages
http://www.money-pages.com

Morgan Stanley
http://www.ms.com

Mudit's Trading Desk
http://www.bestcom/~mwahal/invest

Mutual Fund Research
http://www.webcom.com/fundlink

Mutual Funds Magazine On-line
http://www.mfmag.com

Netscape
http://www.netscape.com

NETworth
http://networth.galt.com/

100% No-Load Mutual Fund Council
http://networth.galt.com.www/home/mutual/100/100dirmf.htm

Onramp Access Stocks and Commodities
http://www.onr.com/stocks.html

OpenText
http://www.opentext.com

PAWWS Financial Network
http://pawws.secapl.com/

PC Quote
http://www.pcquote.com

PR Newswire
http://www.prnewswire.com

Quote.com
http://www.quote.com

Salomon Brothers
http://www.salomon.com

Securities and Exchange Commission
http://www.sec.gov

Silicon Investor
http://www.techstocks.com/

Stock Research Group
http://www.stockgroup.com

The Syndicate
http://moneypages.com/syndicate/

Tile.Net
http://www.tile.net/tile/news/index.html

T. Rowe Price
http://www.troweprice.com

URouLette
http://www.uroulette.com

Vanguard
http://www.vanguard.com

The Wall Street Journal Money and Investing Update
http://update.wsj.com/

WebCrawler
http://www.webcrawler.com

Web Investor Dictionary
http://home.gwp.com/wmartin/dict.html

The Whole Internet Catalog Personal Finance Page
http://www.gnn.com/gnn/wic/wics/persfin.new.html

World Bank
http://www.worldbank.org

Yahoo!
http://www.yahoo.com

Zacks Investment Research
http://aw.zacks.com

Newsgroups

Here is a list of newsgroups that address investment-related issues:

Accounting
biz.comp.accounting

pdaxs.services.accounting

relcom.accounting

Asset Management Topics
misc.invest.asset-management

Banking
aol.news.business.services.banking

Emerging Markets
misc.invest.emerging

Finance
alt.building.finance

fedreg.finance

gwu.msfinance

tw.bbs.sci.finance

uk.finance

Fixed-Income Investment Topics
misc.invest.fixed-income

Foreign Exchange
misc.invest.forex

Futures
misc.invest.futures

Indexed Futures
misc.invest.index-futures

Investing in Commodities
misc.invest.commodities

Investments, General Discussion
misc.invest

alt.invest

alt.invest.penny-stocks

alt.invest.real-estate

alt.private.investigator

aol.news.market.stocks.det

asu.investigates.info-highway

aus.invest

misc.invest.stocks

misc.invest.stocks.penny

relcom.commerce.stocks

realtynet.invest

alt.invest.penny-stocks

Investment Topics Relating to Canada
misc.invest.canada

Money and Money Management
acc.sbell.ushead.money

alt.community.local-money

americast.ushead.money

aol.news.market.money-currency

fj.life.money

microsoft.public.money

relcom.commerce.money

ukr.commerce.money

Mutual Funds and Other Investment Funds
mist.invest.funds

News
Administeringnews.news.adm

New York Stock Exchange
info.nysersnmp

ny.nysernet

ny.nysernet.map

ny.nysernet.maps

ny.nysernet.nic

ny.nysernet.nysertech

sfnet.lists.nysersnmp

Options Investment
misc.invest.options

Penny Stocks
misc.invest.stocks.penny

Precious Metals
misc.invest.precious-metals

Real Estate
misc.invest.real-estate

Retirement, Aging Gerontology
soc.retirement

Stocks
alt.invest.penny-stocks

aol.news.market.stocks.details

misc.invest.stocks

relcom.commerce.stocks

Technical Analysis for Investors
misc.invest.technical

Mutual Funds

Many Web sites contain mutual fund information. Here are some to try out:

AAL Mutual Funds
http://www.aal.org/index.html

Alger
http://networth.galt.com/alger/

American Heritage
http://networth.galt.com/www/home/mutual/100/american/

Ameristock
http://www.ameristock.com

AmSouth
e-mail: aso hsv@ro.comhttp://www.ro.com/pages/amsouth

Analytic Investment Management
http://networth.galt.com/www/home/mutual/100/analytic/

Armstrong Associates
http://networth.galt.com/www/home/mutual/100/armstrong

ASM
http://networth.galt.com/www/home/mutual/100/asm

Astrologers Fund
http://www.ids.net/starbridge/afund/

Avondale Total Return Fund
http://networth.galt.com/www/home/mutual/100/avondale

Babson Funds
http://networth.galt.com/babson/

Bank of America
http://www.bankamerica.com

Benham Group
http://networth.galt.com/benham/

Calvert Group
http://www.calvertgroup.com/

Century Shares Trust
http://networth.galt.com/www/home/mutual/100/century/

C/Funds Group, Inc.
http://networth.galt.com/www/home/mutual/100/cfunds

Citizens Trust
http://www.efund.com

Eclipse Funds
http://networth.galt.com/www/home/mutual/100/eclipse/

Fairmont Fund
http://networth.galt.com/www/home/mutual/100/fairmont

Fasciano Fund
http://networth.galt.com/www/home/mutual/100/fasciano/

Federated Investors
http://networth.galt.com.www/home/mutual/federated

Fidelity Investors
http://www.fid-inv.com/

First Union
http://www.firstunion.
com/services/brokerage.
html

Gabelli Funds
http://www.gabelli.com/

GAM Funds
http://www.usinfo.
gam.com/

GIT Investment Funds
http://www.gitfunds.
com/

Hambrecht & Quist
http://www.hamquist.
com/

Hudson Investors Fund
http://www.greenmoney.
com/hudson/index.htm

IAI Mutual Funds
http://networth.galt.com.
iai/

ICAP Funds
http://networth.galt.com/
www/home/mutual/
100/icap/

INVESCO Funds Group
http://www.invesco.com/

Janus Funds
http://networth.galt.com/
www/home/mutual/
janus/

Jones & Babson Group
http://networth.galt.com/
babson

Kaufmann Fund
http://networth.galt.com/
kaufmann/

Kemper Fund Group
http://www.kemper.
com/

Lebenthal
http://www.lebenthal.
com/

**Legg Mason Family of
Funds**
http://www.leggmason.
com/Funds

**Liberty Asset
Management Co.**
http://www.lib.com/
LAMCO/lamco.html

Lindner Funds
http://networth.galt.com/
www/home/mutual/
lindner/

Loomis Sayles Funds
http://networth.galt.com/
loomis/

Markman MultiFunds
http://http://networth.
galt.com/www/home/
mutual/100/markman

Mark Twain Funds
http://www.marktwain.
com/

MassMutual
http://www.
massmutual.com/

Montgomery Funds
http://networth.galt.com/
mntgmry/

Muhlenkamp Fund
http://networth.galt.com/
www/home/mutual/100/
muhlenkamp/

Munder Funds
http://www.munder.
com/funds.html

New England Funds
http://www.
mutualfunds.com/

**Newport Pacific
Management**
http://www.lib.com/
newport/newport.html

Nicholas Family of Funds
http://www.secapl.com/
pub/webster/nac/
nac.html

Norwest
http://www.norwest.
com/

Numeric Investors
http://www.numeric.
com/

Oak Value Funds
http://networth.galt.com/
www/home/
mutual/100/oak/

PaxWorld
http://greenmoney.com/
pax/

PBHG Funds
http://networth.galt.com/
www/home/mutual/
100/pbhg/

**Peregrine Asset
Management**
http://networth.galt.com/
www/home/mutual/
100/peregrine/

Piper Jaffray
http://www.piperjaffray.
com/money_
management/

Primary Funds
http://networth.galt.com/
www/home/mutual/100/
primary/

Principal
http://www.principal.
com/about/know9.html

Prudent Bear Fund
http://www.tice.com/
PRUDBEAR.htm

**Robertson, Stephens &
Co.**
http://www.rsco.com/
mf/mutual.htm

Royce Funds
http://networth.galt.com/
www/home/mutual/
royce/

SAFECO Mutual Funds
http://networth.galt.com/
www/home/mutual/100/
safeco/

Seafirst
http://seafirst.com/
bank

Selected Family of Funds
http://networth.galt.
com/selected/

Sit Mutual Fund Group
http://networth.galt.com/
www/home/mutual/
100/sit

Solon Funds
http://networth.galt.com/
www/home/
mutual/100/solon/

State Street Boston Corp.
http://www.statestreet.
com/

Stein Roe Mutual Funds
http://www.steinroe.com

Stratton Funds
http://networth.galt.com/
www/home/
mutual/100/stratton/

TIAA-CREF
http://www.tiaa-cref.org/

Transamerica
http://www.
transamerica.com/

**Twentieth Century
Mutual Funds**
http://networth.galt.
com/twntyth/

Union Investors Funds
http://www.
careersmosaic.com/cm/
union_bank/ub2.html#E
**United Group of Mutual
Funds**
http://www.waddell.
com/ugmf.htm

United Services Funds
http://www.usfunds.
com/

**Van Kampen American
Capital**
http://www.vkac.com/

**Variable Annuity Life
Insurance Companies
(VALIC)**
http://chronicle.merit.
edu/.vendors/.valic/.
home.html

Volumetric Fund
http://networth.galt.com/
www/home/mutual/100/
volumetric/

Vontobel Funds
http://networth.galt.com/
www/home/mutual/100/
vontobel/

**Waddell & Reed Mutual
Funds**
http://www.waddell.
com/wrf.htm

Wayne Hummer Funds
http://networth.galt.com/
www/home/mutual/100/
wayne

Wright Investors' Funds
http://networth.galt.com/
www/home/mutual/
wright/

**Zeske, Sarafa, &
Associates**
http://www.zsa.com/

Zweig Mutual Funds
http://networth.galt.com/
www/home/mutual/
zweig

Index

New CD-ROM Money Maker Kits from Dearborn Multimedia

Book & CD-ROM Set

A DEARBORN MONEY MAKER KIT

THE MORTGAGE KIT
THIRD EDITION

SELECT THE RIGHT LOAN
NEGOTIATE THE BEST TERMS
LOCK IN THE LOWEST RATE
UNDERSTAND ALL YOUR OPTIONS

THOMAS C. STEINMETZ
PHILLIP WHITT

Features:

- *25 minute video help with the author*
- *12-28 interactive printable forms per CD-ROM*
- *On-Line glossary of terms*
- *Quick-start video tutorial*
- *Interactive printable book on CD-ROM*
  (Print out sections you like for closer reading or writing notes.)

Start Enjoying Greater Financial Freedom
Triple Your Investment Portfolio

SAVE Thousands on Real Estate as a Buyer or Seller

Real Estate

The Homebuyer's Kit
Find the Right House Fast

With this multimedia kit:
- Negotiate with confidence
- Prequalify using the automated formulas to determine your best mortgage terms
- Chart your progress using the interactive home comparison forms

Order No. 1800-0401
$34.95

More than 10 million readers watch for **Edith Lank's** award-winning real estate column, *"House Calls"*.

The Homeseller's Kit
Get Top Dollar When Selling Your Home

With this multimedia kit:
- Sell your home for more $
- Understand the tax consequences of selling
- Identify low-cost fix-up tips that add value to your home
- Negotiate your contract with confidence to get the best offer

Order No. 1800-4601
$34.95

More than 10 million readers watch for Edith Lank's award-winning real estate column, *"House Calls"*.

The Mortgage Kit
Save Big $$$ When Financing Your Home

With this multimedia kit:
- Select the right loan
- Lock in the best interest rate
- Prequalify using the automated forms and checklists
- Determine how much money you will save when refinancing
- Organize your mortgage search using the interactive checklists

Order No. 1800-2201
$34.95

Thomas C. Steinmetz was a senior strategic planner with the Federal National Mortgage Association.
Phillip Whitt has worked 12 years in residential mortgage lending.

The Homeowner's Kit
The Homeowner's Kit Will Help You Protect Your Most Valuable Asset—Your Home!

With this multimedia kit:
- Save money and conserve energy
- Refinance for the lowest rates

Just point and click to discover:
- Hundreds of home safety and security tips
- How to inspect your home

Order No. 1800-1901
$34.95

Robert de Heer is a professional real estate author who simplifies home-owning with specific money saving steps.

The Home Inspection Kit
Uncover the Secrets of Money-Saving Home Inspections and Protect the Safety of Your Family

With this multimedia kit:
- Oversee the more than 349 points of a thorough inspection using the automated Master Inspection Checklist
- Choose the most profitable remodeling projects at the click of your mouse.

Over 30,000 Copies Sold!

Order No. 1800-3101
$34.95

William Ventolo, Jr., MS, has years of experience as an educational publishing executive and consultant.

Careers

Top Secret Resumes & Cover Letters

With this multimedia kit:
- Access expert resume coaching from a veteran with a 4,000+ resume track record
- Choose the most effective format, layout, and typefaces
- Find easy-to-use access to the most effective words and phrases
- Get expert answers to the most-asked resume questions

Order No. 1800-4001, $34.95

Steven Provenzano has written over 4,000 resumes and owns A Advanced Resume Service, Inc.

Successfully Start & Manage a <u>NEW</u> Business

··· Small Business ···

The Business Planning Guide
Plan for Success in Your New Venture

With this multimedia kit:
- Just plug in your financials to plan your dream business
- Point and click to automate planning and financial forecasts
- Start, expand, or buy a business

Order No. 1800-0101
$34.95

David H. Bangs, Jr. is founder of Upstart Publishing Company, Inc.

How To Form Your Own Corporation Without a Lawyer For Under $75

With this multimedia kit:
- Save thousands of dollars in legal fees
- Limit your personal liability and protect your assets
- Access the complete set of forms, certificate of incorporation, minutes, and more

Order No. 1800-1601
$34.95

Ted Nicholas owns and operates four corporations of his own and acts as a consultant to small businesses.

Starting Your Home-Based Business
39 Million People Can't Be Wrong

With this multimedia kit:
- Position your home-based business for long-term success
- Deal effectively with zoning, labor laws, and licenses
- Answers to the 20 most-asked questions

Order No. 1800-2801
$34.95

Linda Pinson and **Jerry Jinnett** are consultants and speakers as well as successful business owners and authors.

The Start-Up Guide
Everything You Need to Create a Smart Start in Your New Business

With this multimedia kit:
- Create your own 12-month interactive start-up plan
- Access interactive management, bookkeeping, and marketing forms
- Learn the best ways to deal with bankers, vendors, and investors
- Get the financing you need

Order No. 1800-1001
$34.95

David H. Bangs, Jr. is a frequent speaker and acknowledged expert on small business management topics.

---

3 Easy Ways to Order

1. By Mail:
Mail to:
Dearborn Multimedia
155 N. Wacker Drive
Chicago, IL 60606

2. By FAX:
FAX your order
(with credit card information)
to: 1-312-836-9958

3. By Phone:
Call Toll-Free
(credit card orders only)
1-800-638-0375
Have your Visa, MasterCard, or American Express handy.

Name_____

Address_____ City_____

State_____ Zip_____ Phone (   )_____

❏ Personal Check Enclosed (checks payable to: Dearborn Financial Publishing)

Credit Card Information   ❏ Visa   ❏ MasterCard   ❏ AMEX

Account #_____ Exp. Date_____

Signature_____

Order No.	Title	Price	Qty.	Total

Subtotal	
Sales Tax (CA, FL, IL and NY only)	
Shipping & Handling $5.00	
Total	

Dearborn Multimedia
155 North Wacker Drive
Chicago, IL 60606
1-800-638-0375   Source Code 605119